THE SPIRIT OF THE GARDEN

AMERICAN SOCIETY OF LANDSCAPE ARCHITECTS
CENTENNIAL REPRINT SERIES

Editors:

Charles A. Birnbaum, FASLA, National Park Service,
Historic Landscape Initiative, Washington, D.C.

Catherine Howett, ASLA, School of Environmental Design,
University of Georgia, Athens, Georgia

Marion Pressley, FASLA, Pressley Associates,
Cambridge, Massachusetts

David C. Streatfield, Royal Institute for British Architects,
University of Washington, Seattle, Washington

ASLA CENTENNIAL REPRINT SERIES

*Country Life: A Handbook of Agriculture and Book of
Landscape Gardening* (1866)
Robert Morris Copeland

Landscape Architecture as Applied to the Wants of the West (1873)
H. W. S. Cleveland

Charles Eliot, Landscape Architect (1902)
Charles W. Eliot

The Art of Landscape Architecture (1915)
Samuel Parsons Jr.

Prairie Spirit in Landscape Gardening (1915)
Wilhelm Miller

Landscape-Gardening (1920)
O. C. Simonds

The Spirit of the Garden (1923)
Martha Brookes Hutcheson

Book of Landscape Gardening (1926)
Frank Waugh

New Towns for Old (1927)
John Nolen

Landscape for Living (1950)
Garrett Eckbo

The series is underwritten by the Viburnum Foundation.

THE SPIRIT OF THE GARDEN

MARTHA BROOKES HUTCHESON

Introduction by
Rebecca Warren Davidson

University of Massachusetts Press
AMHERST

in association with

Library of American Landscape History
AMHERST

Introduction to this edition © 2001 by Rebecca Warren Davidson

This volume is reprinted from the first edition of *The Spirit of the Garden,*
published by The Atlantic Monthly Press in 1923.

Printed in the United States of America
LC 00–048879
ISBN 1–55849–272–0
Printed and bound by Sheridan Books, Inc.

Library of Congress Cataloging-in-Publication Data

Hutcheson, Martha Brookes Brown, 1871–1959
The spirit of the garden / Martha Brookes Hutcheson ; introduction by Rebecca Warren Davidson.
p. cm. — (American Society of Landscape Architects Centennial reprint series)
Originally published: Boston: Atlantic Monthly Press, 1923.
"In association with Library of American Landscape History."
Includes bibliographical references.
ISBN 1–55849–272–0 (alk. paper)
1. Landscape gardening. I. Library of American Landscape History. II. Title.
III. Centennial reprint series.

SB472 .H85 2000
712—dc21
00–048879

British Library Cataloguing in Publication data are available.

PREFACE

The ASLA Centennial Reprint Series comprises a small library of influential historical books about American landscape architecture. The titles were selected by a committee of distinguished editors who identified them as classics, important in shaping design, planting, planning, and stewardship practices in the field and still relevant today. Each is reprinted from the original edition and introduced by a new essay that provides historical and contemporary perspective. The project was undertaken by the Library of American Landscape History to commemorate the 1999 centennial of the American Society of Landscape Architects. The series is funded by the Viburnum Foundation, Rochester, New York.

The Spirit of the Garden, the third volume in the series, was first published in 1923, at the apex of the American Country Place Era. It was written by Martha Brookes Hutcheson (1871–1959), one of the first women to receive formal landscape architectural training and to practice professionally in the United States. Hutcheson's lively text is illustrated with evocative photographs of classic, European landscapes alongside many of her own projects, including several of Merchiston Farm, Hutcheson's Gladstone, New Jersey, estate, and Maudsleigh, now a state park in Newburyport, Massachusetts. Rising interest in the significance of Hutcheson's writings and designs is, happily, encouraging preservation of these sites. We are hopeful that the reprinting of *The Spirit of the Garden* will draw attention to other landscapes where the talented designer once worked and encourage similar preservation efforts there.

As did her somewhat better known female colleagues Ellen Biddle Shipman and Beatrix Jones Farrand, Hutcheson believed that Europe, and Italy in particular, offered a model for garden design that would serve American needs if enlivened with a rich, loose planting style. Unlike Farrand and Shipman, however, Hutcheson found the opportunity to put pen to paper and communicate her ideas to a wide and eager general public during one of the most intense gardening episodes in the history of the United States. As Rebecca Warren Davidson points out in her new introduction, *The Spirit of the Garden* was one of the few books of its day to address the garden as a spatial as well as horticultural entity. In Davidson's view, Hutcheson's book was also a historically significant work, an expression of the Progressive Era notion that landscape architecture could be a force for civic betterment.

Hutcheson retired from active practice in 1912, after the birth of her only child. During the course of her brief career, she laid out over fifty gardens, few of which survive intact today. Although she continued to write and lecture about the importance of good design—and was made a Fellow of the ASLA in 1935—her reputation was quietly obscured. "That despite these significant achievements Hutcheson is little known today," Davidson explains, "has to do in part with the way we have written our history and in part with how she chose to conduct her life. . . . The smaller, domestic garden in the United States was generally left to the care of women, and the work of those who did create successful careers for themselves as designers, photographers, and writers focusing on these small private spaces has been marginalized because of its perceived lack of social relevance as well as its association with 'women's work.'" Davidson's essay seeks to correct history's oversight, examining Hutcheson's background, education, and her written and built contributions to the field. She also analyzes the author's complex motives in writing *The Spirit of the Garden* and briefly examines links to other books that Hutcheson's may have influenced.

Home gardeners will be inspired by Hutcheson's sound advice, transporting photographs, and lyrical prose. In one memorable passage, she writes of an old, abandoned garden that "through its truancy lends the gayety of poppies to the melon patch and of morning-glories to the bean poles." Hutcheson's graceful text reminds readers that fine landscape architecture depends not only on firm principles but also on art, rooted in sympathetic understanding of the land.

To vitalize the connection between Hutcheson's book and land stewardship today, Library of American Landscape History has invited four sites with elements of gardens designed by Hutcheson to join us as educational partners in celebrating the reprint's publication: Bamboo Brook Outdoor Education Center, Gladstone, New Jersey (formerly Hutcheson's home, Merchiston Farm); National Park Service Longfellow National Historic Site, Cambridge, Massachusetts; National Park Service Marsh-Billings-Rockefeller National Historical Park, Woodstock, Vermont; and Maudslay State Park, Newburyport, Massachusettts (formerly Maudesleigh, the Frederick S. Moseley estate).

Robin Karson, Executive Director
Library of American Landscape History
Amherst, Massachusetts

LIBRARY of

AMERICAN
LANDSCAPE
HISTORY

Library of American Landscape History, Inc., a nonprofit organization, produces books and exhibitions about American landscape history. Its mission is to educate and thereby promote thoughtful stewardship of the land.

INTRODUCTION
TO THE REPRINT EDITION

REBECCA WARREN DAVIDSON

When *The Spirit of the Garden* appeared in 1923, the number of books already available brimming with advice for the amateur gardener might have daunted a less assured writer.[1] Martha Brookes Hutcheson (fig. 1), however, was confident that her book would find a place on the shelves of many newly prosperous, upwardly mobile Americans who were avidly seeking advice on homebuilding, decorating, and especially gardening. Her contribution offered something unique: a straightforward articulation of the basic, architectural principles of the design of space and their application in the small garden, combined with an enthusiastic and knowledgeable advocacy of the use of native plants.

History has proved Hutcheson correct. *The Spirit of the Garden* has continued to be read and valued, not only for its clear explanation of landscape design concepts but also for Hutcheson's ideas on the social and cultural importance of gardens to individuals and to their communities. Until now, though, only the persevering reader fortunate enough to find a copy in a library or used bookstore has had the opportunity to appreciate Hutcheson's insights. With the publication of this reprint that situation is happily changed.

The Spirit of the Garden is much more than a historic document in the literature of American landscape architecture, however. It is also arguably the most significant and tangible legacy of one of the first women to engage in the professional practice of landscape architecture in the United States. The skill and knowledge Hutcheson accumulated over the course of her professional life is summarized in the book, which showcases—with her own photographs—the best of the more than fifty private gardens she designed and built during her career.[2]

In addition to her accomplishments as a designer, Hutcheson was for more than forty years a successful author and lecturer on the importance of good design as a force for social and civic betterment. In 1935, the American Society of Landscape Architects recognized her contributions by making her a Fellow of the Society, only the third woman to be so honored. That despite these significant achievements Hutcheson is little known today has to do in part with the way we have written our history and in part with how she chose to conduct her life. The fact that Hutcheson's active career lasted a relatively

vii

Figure 1. Martha Brookes Hutcheson. Charcoal sketch by
Jane de Glehn, 1922. *Morris County Park Commission.*

short time—her first documented work was in 1901, and she seems, by her own choice,
to have built little after her marriage in 1910—certainly has affected her place in our
collective memory. That her work, almost without exception, consisted of private, domestic gardens for wealthy northeasterners is also a contributing factor, but one over which
she would have had little control. The design of large-scale landscape projects was the
nearly exclusive purview of men in early twentieth-century America,[3] and their built
works—urban parks, cemeteries, parkways, and subdivisions—have also, quite naturally,
been the focus of most previous historical research. The smaller, domestic garden in the

Figure 2. Martha Brookes Brown and William Anderson Hutcheson and their wedding party at Fern Hill, near Burlington, Vermont, 12 October 1910. *Morris County Park Commission.*

United States was generally left to the care of women, and the work of those who did create successful careers for themselves as designers, photographers, and writers focusing on these small private spaces has been marginalized because of its perceived lack of social relevance as well as its association with "women's work." Despite previous neglect, however, more recent scholarship is beginning to amass an impressive record of documentation and analysis showing the importance of the domestic garden as a signifier of social structures and relationships and of American cultural and aesthetic aspirations.[4]

Martha Brookes Brown Hutcheson[5] was born in New York City on 2 October 1871, a time when no formal education in landscape architecture—or, indeed, the profession itself as such—existed. Hutcheson grew up in a family of avid gardeners, and as an adult she recalled among her earliest pleasurable experiences working in the gardens and fields of her great-uncle John Pomeroy's farm, Fern Hill, near Burlington, Vermont, where her family spent every summer (fig. 2).[6] From 1893 to 1895 she attended the

Figure 3. Sketch of "Roses" made while Martha Brookes Brown was a student at the New York School of Applied Design for Women, ca. 1895. *Morris County Park Commission.*

New York School of Applied Design for Women, although whether she actually aspired to be a decorative artist is unknown.[7] Her studies there included mechanical drawing, the history of ornament, and the creation of designs for book covers and fabrics (fig. 3).[8] Hutcheson also took private instruction in watercolors from the English American painter and writer Rhoda Holmes Nicholls.[9] Like many other young people of the day with the means to do so, she augmented her formal education by undertaking the American equivalent of the grand tour, studying and making notes on gardens in England, France, and Italy during the late 1890s.

The year 1900 was a pivotal moment in Hutcheson's life, as well as a critical juncture in the history of formal instruction in landscape design in the United States. That fall the country's first academic programs in landscape architecture were instituted, at Harvard (as an independent department) and at the Massachusetts Institute of Technology (as part of the Department of Architecture), and Hutcheson enrolled in MIT's. Harvard's program was restricted to male applicants only;[10] at MIT, although official policy did not exclude them, women found gaining admission difficult because of their lack of opportunity to study the mathematics and sciences that were vital parts of the entrance requirements and the curriculum. Hutcheson's contemporary at MIT, Marian Cruger Coffin (1876–1957), paints a vivid picture of what the program was like for women:

> You can imagine how terrifying such an institution as "Tech" appeared to a young woman who had never gone more than a few months to a regular school, and when it was reluctantly dragged from me that I had had only a smattering [of] algebra and hardly knew the meaning of the word "geometry," the authorities turned from me in calm contempt. . . . I was told that I was totally unprepared to take the course and refused admittance. It was owing to his [Professor Chandler's] kindness and also to Professor Sargent's and Mr. Lowell's encouragement that I persevered and was able by intensive tutoring in mathematics to be admitted as a "special" student in Landscape Architecture, taking all the technical studies and combining the first two years in one so that I finished in three years.[11]

Ironically, if Hutcheson had delayed her studies just one more year, she would have been able to take advantage of a program founded exclusively for women at the Lowthorpe School of Landscape Architecture and Horticulture in Groton, Massachusetts, in 1901. And beginning in 1915, a handful of intrepid female students would persuade Harvard instructors Henry Atherton Frost and Bremer Pond to tutor them privately in another program that would eventually become the Cambridge School of Architectural and Landscape Design for Women.[12] Both these options were unavailable, however, when Hutcheson was considering what she should do for her life's work. Undoubtedly her family expected her to marry or perhaps pursue a career in the decorative arts, but Hutcheson had other ideas, as she later recalled:

> About 1898, one day I saw the grounds of Bellevue Hospital in New York, on which nothing was planted, and was overcome with the terrible waste of opportunity for beauty which was not being given to the hundreds of patients who could see it or go to it, in convalescence. In trying to find out how I could get in touch with such authorities as those who might allow me to plant the area of ground, I stumbled upon the fact that my aim would be politically impossible, but that there was a course in Landscape Architecture being formed at the Massachusetts Institute of Technology, the first course which America had ever held. After a conference with those in connection with this training, and with Mrs. Farrand, who was then practicing alone in the field, I was fired with the desire to enter the Institute . . . [and] I began at once to study the mathematics which were required for entrance, and to put my private-school-tutored mind into as good shape as I could on the various subjects before entering the second year of the course.[13]

INTRODUCTION

These remarks reveal one of Hutcheson's primary motivations in becoming a landscape architect—to be able to bring about positive social changes through landscape design. In this desire, Hutcheson allied herself with the activists of the Progressive Era in early twentieth-century America—reform-minded individuals and groups who tried to identify and to solve the widespread social problems of a rapidly industrializing nation. Some of these reformers even believed that the garden itself was an effective instrument of social change, particularly useful for its "civilizing" effects, not only on the impoverished and on recently arrived immigrants but also on members of the middle class who had higher social aspirations.[14]

The idea of social reform through landscape architecture was present in Hutcheson's mind from the beginning of her career, and it informed her writings throughout her life. Judging by the published curriculum, however, it was not part of the MIT approach. An architect, Guy Lowell (1870–1927), headed the MIT program and had also been largely responsible for designing the course of instruction. Today Lowell is best known for his 1902 book, *American Gardens*, which documented the beginnings of the formal garden revival in the United States and showcased the new, often elaborate examples created by architects for their wealthy clients.[15] In his own day, however, Lowell was known primarily for his cultural and civic buildings such as Boston's Museum of Fine Arts and the New York County Courthouse. A graduate of Harvard and the MIT School of Architecture, in 1900 Lowell had just returned from five years in Paris, where he had been awarded the *diplôme* in architecture from the Ecole des Beaux-Arts and had also studied landscape design with Edouard André, superintendent of the city's parks and professor at the Ecole National d'Horticulture de Versailles.[16]

Given Lowell's own academic preparation, therefore, it is not surprising that MIT's program strongly emphasized the architectural and scientific aspects of landscape design, with courses such as perspective and topographical drawing, geometry, physics, and structural geology composing a major portion of the curriculum. Only in the second term of the fourth (and final) year was any requirement listed which focused on the social importance of landscape architecture: a course in public health and sanitation.[17] Although horticulture was offered in each term of the second, third, and fourth years, Hutcheson clearly found MIT's program inadequate in this respect, and later wrote, "I saw at once that the curriculum did not give nearly enough time to what must be known of the plant world." Accordingly, she took the course of lectures offered by Professor Watson at the Bussey Institution of the Arnold Arboretum and made further studies at local commercial nurseries to "note periods of bloom, combinations in color, variety of species in flowers, and the effects of perennials after blooming."[18]

Hutcheson left MIT in 1902 without taking a degree. She was obviously dissatisfied with the curriculum, but she may also have had personal or professional disagreements with Lowell.[19] In any case, the fact that Hutcheson opened her own office in Boston that same year without serving an apprenticeship, as most men would have done, may be taken as an indication both of her independent spirit and of the prejudice against women entering the field at this time. Her experience was undoubtedly similar to that of Marian Coffin, who later recalled: "On leaving school one expected the world would welcome newly fledged landscape artists, but alas, few people seemed to know what it was all about, while the idea of taking a woman into an office was unheard of. 'My dear young lady, what *will* you do about supervising the work on the ground,' became such a constant and discouraging query that the only thing seemed to be for me to hang out my own shingle and see what I *would* do about it."[20]

Establishing a clientele as a woman landscape professional could not have been easy for Hutcheson,[21] although it seems likely that she had adequate resources from her family to support her during her years of education and early professional practice. Many beginning designers—both male and female—had family and friends who helped in gaining early commissions, and although no proof of it has so far been found, Hutcheson probably did too. Her training at MIT and informal work at the Arnold Arboretum would likely have provided introductions to early clients in the Boston area, such as Charles Head, for whom she designed the entrance drive, garden, and terraces at his home in Prides Crossing, Massachusetts, in 1901. Hutcheson also worked for Frederick S. Moseley at his estate, Maudesleigh, in Newburyport, Massachusetts. There Hutcheson created a number of gardens, redesigned the approach drive to the house, and made various other changes to the landscape over a period of some twenty years. Moseley also consulted the Arnold Arboretum's director, Charles Sprague Sargent, for landscape advice at about the same time he employed Hutcheson.

Because of its size and visibility within the community of wealthy New England garden builders, Maudesleigh was a tremendously important commission for Hutcheson. It is also significant as one of the few remaining Hutcheson designs in any degree intact today and open to the public. Although the house is no longer extant, the drives and gardens she designed for it are now part of Maudslay State Park. Hutcheson included twenty-four photographs of Maudesleigh in *The Spirit of the Garden*—more than of any other design— and she considered her work there to be among her best efforts.

Hutcheson's career also benefited from exposure through the media. Like Guy Lowell, she wrote and published her first theories of landscape design concurrently with her first professional commission. The 1901 issue of *The Cosmopolitan* magazine featured her article "The Garden Spirit," an overview of the history of the garden with a strong emphasis on its spiritual and evocative associations.[22] In 1909, Hutcheson found an opportunity to talk directly to "common men and women" about the principles of domestic garden design in a "conversation" with the editor of *The Outlook* magazine, illustrated with photographs of her own work.[23] Substantial material from both these articles, as well as several others that were published in *The House Beautiful*,[24] later appeared as chapters in *The Spirit of the Garden*, evidence that Hutcheson's philosophy of design was developed early in her career and remained consistent.

Hutcheson's life changed significantly after her marriage in 1910 to William Anderson Hutcheson, an actuary who had emigrated to the United States from Scotland and who eventually became a vice president of the Mutual Life Insurance Company of New York. In 1911, they purchased a summer home near Gladstone, New Jersey, consisting of an eighteenth-century farmhouse and one hundred acres of land. Following the birth of their only child, Martha, in 1912, Hutcheson made the development of the house and landscape at Merchiston Farm—named after the school William had attended in Edinburgh—her primary design concern. For the next forty years she continued to experiment and refine the gardens and surrounding landscape at her home. Today in the care of the Morris County Park Commission as Bamboo Brook Outdoor Education Center, it offers one of the best opportunities for the public to experience Hutcheson's built work and understand her design intentions in three-dimensional form.

Except for her own domestic environment and her work for a few clients for whom, in her own words, she continued to act as a "consulting landscape gardener," Hutcheson's professional focus shifted in midlife from designing and building gardens to lecturing and writing about them. By remaining active in the ASLA, however, and by acting as an occasional visiting critic at the Lowthorpe School, Hutcheson did maintain some professional contacts and exerted an influence on a younger generation of landscape architects as well.[25]

In 1913, Hutcheson became a founding member of the Somerset Hills (New Jersey) affiliate of the Garden Club of America and gave numerous lectures, both under its auspices and independently. The archive of her papers contains numerous drafts of public lectures she delivered but which remain unpublished. Two examples, both given in prominent venues, are "Co-operation of Citizens, Trained and Untrained, in Beautifying Our Rural Towns," presented at the annual meeting of the American Civic Association in Philadelphia, October 1919, and "The Fine Art of Landscape Architecture," at the Metropolitan Museum of Art in 1931. Although she also participated in such typical Garden Club activities as judging flower shows, Hutcheson, not surprisingly, emphasized in her writings and lectures that the organization should be a force for cultural and civic betterment rather than a mere social club.[26] Hutcheson also actively promoted other landscape-related progressive causes. She was one of the founders, for example, of the

Figure 4. Members of the Woman's Land Army at Merchiston Farm, ca. 1918.
Morris County Park Commission.

Woman's Land Army of America, which attempted to alleviate the shortage of farm labor during World War I by employing women (fig. 4).

The Spirit of the Garden is Hutcheson's most complete and mature statement of the philosophy and principles she developed during more than twenty-five years of designing, building, writing, and thinking about gardens. Of particular significance is her emphasis on the garden as a means of creating and delineating space. This focus may have been motivated initially by a desire to distinguish her book from the many other gardening manuals on the market, but it also accorded closely with her own theoretical stance. As Hutcheson observes in her foreword, there already existed a proliferation of literature that provided "comprehensive and helpful planting-charts, color-schemes and lists of valuable varieties of plants"—information, in other words, to enable the amateur to create interesting and attractive set pieces of garden art. What was needed instead—and much more difficult to find, she claimed—was an explanation of "the underlying principles of comprehensive planning . . . earnestly looked for by many amateurs, to whom the fact is very clear that all the planting material in the world is of little value if a sense of such basic principles as may be realized by all is lacking."

Hutcheson's concern with the architecture of the garden was highlighted by Ernest Peixotto, the artist and architectural draftsman who wrote the introduction to the book. In addition to praising her "restrained tone and the sober spirit of her text," Peixotto associated Hutcheson's work with the classic gardens of Europe and with eighteenth-century colonial gardens, which in the early twentieth century were the focus of much American historical and nostalgic interest. Peixotto includes Hutcheson in that "small group of landscape gardeners, worthy of the name, [who have recently] brought back our thoughts to a real consideration of design as applied to the art of garden-planning."

In her foreword, Hutcheson identifies two themes of particular importance. One is her belief in the spiritual and social importance of the garden. By dedicating her book "to those with a *progressive spirit* in their concern for the fine art of garden making," she seems to be linking her work with that of the reform activists of the Progressive Era, who sought to improve the lives of immigrants, the poor, and even the middle class by providing them with information to raise their standards of taste, gentility, and learning. Hutcheson reinforces this connection by explaining that one of her goals in writing the book was to give her readers a "conception of the underlying principles of comprehensive planning," to help them improve their "tastes and perceptions" regarding the landscape, in order to "advance . . . our standard of fine gardens and general plantings." In other words, she wanted not only to improve her readers' lives through their involvement in gardening, but also to convey to them—particularly to the aspiring middle class—a specific set of principles based on the best (i.e., elite) models so as to elevate landscape design standards in general.

Hutcheson's belief in landscape architecture as a social force was a topic to which she returned again and again in her writings and lectures. It allies her with earlier, nineteenth-century landscape designers such as Andrew Jackson Downing and Frederick Law Olmsted Sr., who believed wholeheartedly in landscape design as a means of social "improvement," and with her contemporaries who worked in other fields, whose writings addressed not gardens but social issues such as public housing, sanitation, and full employment. By contrast, the writings of Hutcheson's colleagues Marian Coffin and Elsa Rehmann aimed to convey information about both design and practical matters, such as what types of plants should be used in various landscaping situations.[27]

Hutcheson's foreword also encourages her readers to recognize the value of native plants and use them to create attractive and vigorous American gardens. "As a nation," she wrote, "we are just awakening to our wealth [of native plant materials] and our need for conservation of our vast natural beauty with its amazing variety in scene and in plant life." The benefits of using native plants and appreciating native American scenery was a theme Hutcheson reiterated throughout her writings. In an article for the *Garden Club of America Bulletin*, for example, she reminds her readers that "each locality holds its own supply of varied native vegetation tempered to the soil, the moisture and the climate of its environment" and decries the wholesale destruction of this natural wealth for no other reason than homeowners' desire to substitute high-maintenance exotics.[28] Rather, she advised Garden Club members to "learn to know the wealth in plant material which we have," and to encourage by example householders of more modest resources to derive the same landscape benefits—"background, foreground, privacy, incidental shadow, and decorative feature"—from native plants as from "foreign imports."[29]

Although Hutcheson was certainly not the only landscape designer to advocate the use of native plants in ornamental landscaping—Ossian Cole Simonds, Wilhelm Miller, and Jens Jensen worked throughout their careers to foster an appreciation for increased use of regional plant materials—she was among the first to do so in a book of advice for the amateur garden-maker and to promote these ideas within the context of the Garden Club of America. Hutcheson herself may have been particularly influenced by Simonds's book *Landscape-Gardening*, published in 1920, only a few years before her own.[30] In turn, Hutcheson's book likely played a role in increasing general awareness of the value of native plants. By 1929, Elsa Rehmann and botanist Edith Roberts in their book *American Plants for American Gardens* noted and welcomed what they saw as the increasing demand for indigenous plants in garden designs and even for so-called native gardens.[31]

The Spirit of the Garden is divided into six chapters, each illustrated with photographs, most taken by Hutcheson herself. Of these, more than two-thirds are of her own garden designs; the remainder are primarily of Italian gardens, with a few examples from England, India, France, and Spain.[32] Although the gardens pictured—whether designed by Hutcheson or selected from among her favorite Italian models—were often created for wealthy clients with large estates, her text and captions emphasize features that could be carried out on the smaller rural or suburban property. Often using illustrations from her own garden at Merchiston Farm, Hutcheson consistently juxtaposed modest constructions of simple materials alongside more elaborate versions of the same feature, to make the point that the principles of their design, placement, and use were fundamentally similar.

Although its title, "The Flower Garden," implies a narrow topic, the book's first chapter presents most of Hutcheson's general design principles, which are then explained in more detail. The fundamental tenet of her design philosophy, namely, to combine elements of European (and more specifically Italian) design—axes, vistas, and an architectural framework—with the richness and variety of native plant material and a freer planting style, is alluded to in her foreword. "As individuals," she writes, "we are slowly becoming conscious of the value of cultivated and aesthetic knowledge in adapting to our home surroundings the good principles in planning which have been handed down to us from the Old World." To this emphasis on the importance of studying historical precedent and reshaping the best of this legacy in contemporary gardens, Hutcheson added three guiding principles: the necessity of a strong relationship between house and garden; the idea of the garden as an "outdoor room" whose hedges, walls, and paths blend the disparate elements of the garden into a harmonious whole; and the use of less structured plantings in more informal areas to blend the garden naturally with the surrounding landscape.

Hutcheson was not, of course, unique in recommending this fusion of architectural structure and informal planting style as an attractive option. The confluence of three distinct styles in late nineteenth- and early twentieth-century garden design contributed to its popularity. The American Colonial Revival combined formal structure with a palette of so-called old-fashioned or grandmother's garden plants, which tended to be naturally looser in conformation and were often left unpruned. The Arts and Crafts garden and the "cottage garden" movements, as seen in the work of such influential designers as Gertrude Jekyll in England and Ellen Biddle Shipman in the United States, also favored this approach to domestic garden design. Finally, Americans' interest in Italian gardens was also a significant factor. Particularly because of the way in which they were viewed and understood in the early twentieth century—in an often overgrown, neglected, or somewhat ruinous state, yet still retaining their basic architectural layout—Italian gardens represented for many designers the ideal marriage of architecture and landscape, art and nature, formality and informality. As Hutcheson herself put it:

> The formality, for example, which is found in the old villa-gardens outside of Rome and on the Tuscan hills is of great interest. . . . they are now but ghosts of their original plan, and the old stone-work is covered with moss that softens every surface. . . . Here, about these old villas, are spots of seclusion, of quiet, of beauty, so near and so personal that one can never tire of them, never cease to wish to go

back again and again; and if that may never be, the thought of them lives in our minds, and we are unsatisfied until we have created in our own land some other spot which at least breathes forth some of their satisfying expression, even if it has not their advantages of great age and tradition as a setting.[33]

It is this ability to create a vivid picture in the minds of her readers, as well as her clear articulation of how to apply the classic, architectural principles of design to the American domestic garden, that makes Hutcheson's writings a unique contribution to early twentieth-century American garden literature.[34]

Hutcheson's narrative and illustrations include many specific examples of how the general principles she defined were to be carried out. The first chapter includes three site plans of gardens designed by her, to illustrate how it might be possible to create a system of logical relationships among house, garden, and surrounding landscape.[35] These relationships not only would "tie everything together" but would also provide what she memorably termed the "reasonable complexity of a garden" (14)—in other words, the variety and interest that can result from revealing controlled vistas or glimpses from one part of the garden into another, making the farther rooms or reaches seem mysterious and inviting.

Hutcheson created a clear set of such house and landscape connections at her own Merchiston Farm, and the sketch plan published in *Spirit* (52) indicates the axes developed to join the house and gardens (*B* and *C*), the orchards (*A*), and water features (*H*) together in a single interlocking composition, with views to the surrounding landscape from the house (*F*) and from the farm quadrangle (*G*). A knowledge of the principle of axis, she claimed, "is as essential to good landscape-gardening as it is to good architecture" (52). At the same time, Hutcheson also wrote convincingly of the value of interrupting axes to good effect in certain situations. As an example of the partial view that allowed tantalizing glimpses of what lay beyond, she used her "restoration" of the gardens at the Craigie-Longfellow house in Cambridge, Massachusetts. The old stable adjacent to the house, she wrote, "lent interest to the garden when seen in part only" (104). Therefore, she built a vine-covered trellis—including an inviting pediment-crowned gate opening—to hide the lower half of the stable and create an enclosure and background for the flower garden. Similarly, she constructed a vine-covered arbor of simple rough poles at Merchiston Farm which served multiple functions: shading a path, concealing much of the working farm from the house and pleasure gardens, and providing attractive views of the weathered buildings (146).

Hutcheson emphasized the importance of the relationship of the garden to the surrounding landscape, as well as between house and garden. The key point, she claimed,

Figure 5. Undercliff, formal garden and pergola.
From Louise Shelton, *Beautiful Gardens in America,* 1924, pl. 45.

is that "formality must spring from formality," in other words, one should not juxtapose natural landscape and garden without some design intervention (13). Her preferred solution was to create a transition zone using "a succession of related approaches" that are axially connected—for example, from a house door to a garden gate, and then perhaps to an orchard, and from there to the entrance to a woodland. Each intervening space should have a mix of features, with architectural elements predominating near the house and more "natural" ones toward the surrounding landscape. The garden Hutcheson designed from 1902 to 1906 for Charles Head at his summer place—then known as Undercliff—on the coast in Manchester, Massachusetts, is a good illustration of this principle.[36]

At Undercliff she was faced with a rocky, steep hill surrounding the house on the land side and the compelling natural seascape of the Atlantic Ocean to the south. As is visible on the plan (11), Hutcheson effected a transition between the garden and the native landscape by building a semicircular arbor covered with luxuriant, rambling "wild" grapevines. At the same time, she tamed the landscape by lowering the grade at the end of the garden eighteen feet and building a retaining wall, which the arbor also disguised (fig. 5). Giving the flower garden its own axis, away from the drama of the ocean, resolved the competition for the viewer's attention between the natural and the designed landscape, and allowed each to be experienced separately. To avoid the fussiness and claustrophobia such a solution might create on a small property, she provided ocean views from the garden, but they were controlled, enframed, and moderated by a low wall; the full panorama of the sea could be appreciated from the wide terrace supporting the house.[37]

Hutcheson faced an even more difficult challenge at Maudesleigh. Both the site of the house and the location of the new garden (with no obvious or coherent relationship to each other) had already been determined by the client.[38] These constraints not only made it impossible to join the garden directly with the house, they necessitated a major project to screen the view of the greenhouses and a water tower north of the garden. Hutcheson's solution was to design a long, curving path from the entrance to the house, which straightened as it approached and again as it left the garden, providing the illusion of axial connection but also an aura of mystery and surprise as it eventually led to "a natural wooded walk of great beauty beyond."[39] Having achieved this atmosphere, Hutcheson created an enclosed garden—analogous to the Italian *giardino segreto*—filled with roses, perennials, arbors, fountain, sundial, and birdbath, and surrounded by a hedge to hide the greenhouses and promote a general feeling of peace and seclusion (figs. 6 and 7). Substantial plantings of native shrubs and trees were also made on the formerly bare hillside between the garden and an unfortunately prominent watertower.

Figure 6. Plan of Maudesleigh, ca. 1902, drawn by Hutcheson.
Morris County Park Commission.

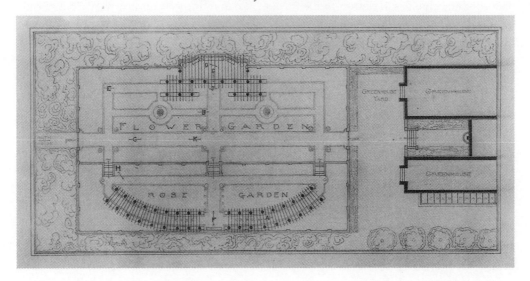

Figure 7. Hutcheson's photograph of the formal garden at Maudesleigh
(corresponds to *D* on the plan). *Morris County Park Commission.*

The resulting changes in view from the formal garden to the greenhouse were dramatically
illustrated in photographs taken by Hutcheson and published in her book (96–100),
showing how the original bare site was transformed into a sheltered space whose arbors
and luxuriant plantings almost totally obscured any intrusion from the outside world,
except through the arched openings cut in the hedge for paths. Hutcheson's other major
achievement at Maudesleigh also affected the relationships among house, gardens, and
landscape. She persuaded her client to relocate the main approach drive from the side
of the house that faced the Merrimack River to the opposite, "land" side, thereby separating the views of the architecture from the most dramatic views of the river, to the advantage of each (fig. 8).

Hutcheson's discussion of the importance of contrast, variety, and mystery in the
garden provides some of her most useful observations on what might be called the
intangible elements of design. She believed, for example, that the designer should
always include some changes in ground level—even if slight and unobtrusive—both

within the garden and between the garden and its surroundings. Well-orchestrated changes in level can be used to give a sense of intimacy to certain chosen spaces, providing contrast and surprise to a walk through the garden. Terracing, steps, and pathways ought to be understood not only as tools for solving the practical problems of getting from one space to another; they also help set the garden apart from both architecture and nature as a distinct and fortunate place. Indeed, the separation of the garden from its surroundings, as "a place apart," was as important to Hutcheson as the connections with them.

What she calls the "green elements" of a garden—trees, shrubs, and hedges—are given their own chapter. They are also, of course, basic structural elements, and here Hutcheson's knowledge and experience of Italian gardens provided her with particularly instructive examples. The hedges at the Boboli Gardens in Florence and the Villa d'Este at Tivoli—

Figure 8. Plan of the forecourt and drive at Maudesleigh, December 1905, drawn by Hutcheson. *Massachusetts Department of Environmental Management.*

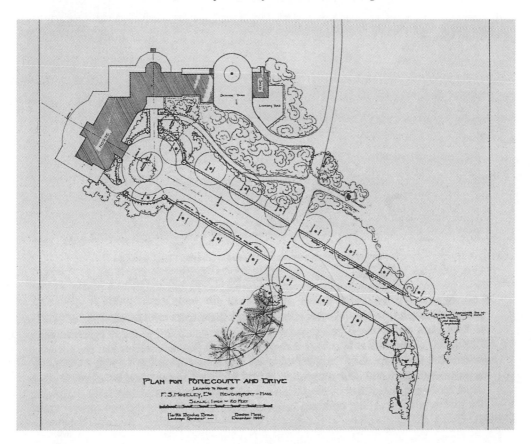

to mention just two of the best examples—are chosen to illustrate how "the green used in the construction of gardens gives us our backgrounds, our contrasts, our proportions, our perspective—above all, our shadows." Hutcheson believed that flowers had been overemphasized in American gardens at the expense of basic structure and form, leading to "too solid a mass of color and too little well-planned green" (15). Her photographs of Maudesleigh prove the effectiveness of her approach. In "A Minor Axis of the Garden," the texture and color of a few perennials are shown to advantage highlighted against dark green masses of shrubs and trees, which lead to a half-open gate in the middle distance (78). The path is continued by steps leading down into another, deliberately unrevealed and mysterious portion of the garden.

The Spirit of the Garden was well received, particularly in art and architecture publications, where many notices praised its clear explication of the basic principles of garden design. In *Architectural Record,* for example, the architect William Lawrence Bottomley wrote that the book was "remarkable for its concise and practical suggestions, its grasp of fundamental principles of garden planning and at the same time, [it is] brilliantly and entertainingly written." He concluded that "every architect who ever does a country place should read it, and every garden lover should have it on a most convenient table."[40] Leila Mechlin, writing in the *American Magazine of Art,* praised the treatment "which is at the same time idealistic and sound" and Hutcheson's clarity—"she interprets accepted theories so that all can understand and put them in practice."[41] Sales were brisk enough to warrant a reprint in 1927, which received notice as well: "First issued in 1923 at a price that limited it to a very few, this classic essay on garden design is now reissued with the same lovely illustrations."[42] Again, reviews were enthusiastic. Edith Heard, in the *Garden Club of America Bulletin,* confessed that "this book has been one of my favorites and it is one of the few I have ever marked, page after page, for my own instruction and for the purposes of quotation."[43]

Although Hutcheson had maintained that her book was neither a practical manual of instruction on how to make a garden nor a substitute for employing the services of a professional landscape designer, nevertheless it clearly filled such a need, particularly for the many Americans in the 1920s who were becoming homeowners for the first time. Similar significant emphasis on the architectural principles of creating a garden was given in a number of books published soon after *The Spirit of the Garden.* For example, Fletcher Steele in his *Design in the Little Garden* of 1924 seems almost to be quoting Hutcheson ("we seldom tie things together enough" [14]) when he writes, "We think too little about tying the landscape organization of the whole place together. . . . all details and parts of a place must be in proper relation to each other and to the whole."[44]

INTRODUCTION

Frank Waugh, also a landscape architect and successful author of books for his colleagues, subtitled his 1927 book, *Formal Design in Landscape Architecture,* "*A Statement of Principles,*" very like Hutcheson's "basic principles as may be realized by all." Of particular interest is the third chapter of Waugh's book, titled "The Domestic Formula," in which he discusses the importance of house and garden relationships; the subdivision of the grounds according to use; delineation of space by walls, hedges, and shrubbery; and circulation systems. Both Waugh and Hutcheson wished to put to rest the formal versus informal controversy that had so preoccupied garden writers of the previous half century. Hutcheson notes that

> an informal path can lead up with so beautiful and dignified a curve . . . that its importance is quite as great as the straight scheme on which we enter the formal garden. If both approaches are carefully planned and planted, one is quite as attractive as the other. The deciding element in the choice lies with the architecture of the house, the lay of the land, and the taste of the owner. (12)

In the same spirit, Waugh maintained that the result of applying his "domestic formula" is

> wholly satisfactory, but it assuredly is not the "natural style"; neither is it the "formal style" as usually expounded. . . . Might it not be a happy ending, therefore, to all controversy about the inherent desirability of formal or natural styles if we could all recognize the simple and significant fact that we have actually developed in America a domestic style of our own which fits our needs, expresses our best taste and is beholden to nobody?[45]

Directions of influence are difficult to define with any certainty, but what can clearly be seen in both these widely read books is a change in the tenor of writing for the amateur garden-maker, emphasizing the architectural and structural aspects of design.

Regrettably little physical evidence remains, but it is clear from the pictorial and written record she left that Martha Brookes Hutcheson was a skillful garden-maker and—perhaps of even more significance—an articulate and influential advocate for good design. Her most important contribution arguably was her understandable articulation of a set of architectural, rational principles of design, expressed both in the gardens she created and in her writings. These principles—the ideal unity of house, garden, and landscape; the garden as an outdoor room, with a structure of walls, hedges, paths, and ornamentation, which could be the focus of a logical planning scheme; and the integration of both formal and informal elements, often through the use of naturalized plantings within an architectural framework—still inform domestic garden-making in the United States today. Although many of her basic ideas were derived from Italian and English traditions, Hutcheson's advocacy of native scenery and her use of local plant materials made her gardens distinctly "American" and helped foster an appreciation for what, even in the early twentieth century, was a rapidly vanishing landscape, succumbing to unchecked industrialization, development, and exploitation. Hutcheson's efforts to educate her readers and clients about garden design and about landscape preservation have gone largely unrecognized since her death. With this republication of her major written work, however, her ideas can once again reach and inspire a wide audience.

Notes

1. Some idea of the amount and variety of this literature may be glimpsed in Anna Gilman Hill, "The Gardener's Miscellany: The Literature of American Gardening," *Garden Club of America Bulletin*, n.s., no. 20 (November 1924): 47–53, and in Stephen F. Hamblin, "Gardening Books for the Client," *Landscape Architecture* 10 (April 1920): 122–23. Hill actually mentions Hutcheson, on p. 53, along with Fletcher Steele and Grace Tabor, as the authors she finds most helpful on the subject of "design." See also Elisabeth Woodburn, "Addendum of Books Published from 1861–1920," in U. P. Hedrick, *A History of Horticulture in America* (Portland, Ore.: Timber Press, 1988): 557–66; and Beverly Seaton, "Gardening Books for the Commuter's Wife, 1900–1937," *Landscape* 28, no. 2 (1985): 41–47.

2. In her application for membership in the American Society of Landscape Architects (ASLA), dated 3 March 1919, Hutcheson stated that during the time she was head of her own office in Boston and New York (1901–1910), "some 83 private places or gardens were laid out from my plans under my supervision." Her "Professional Record," however, lists only 48 clients. Undoubtedly, more gardens designed by Hutcheson remain to be discovered. ASLA application and typescript "Professional Record" are among the papers held in the Martha Brookes Hutcheson Archives, currently in the care of the Morris County Park Commission, Morristown, New Jersey; hereafter cited as MBHA.

3. Some exceptions are Beatrix Farrand's work on the campuses of Princeton and Yale, Ellen Shipman's design for Lake Shore Drive in Grosse Pointe, Michigan, and Marjorie Sewell Cautley's landscaping for such planned developments as Sunnyside Gardens, New York, and Radburn, New Jersey.

4. Recent surveys of private gardens in the United States include Mac Griswold and Eleanor Weller, *The Golden Age of American Gardens* (New York: Abrams, 1991); Peter Martin, *The Pleasure Gardens of Virginia* (Princeton: Princeton University Press, 1991); May Brawley Hill, *Grandmother's Garden: The Old-Fashioned American Garden, 1865–1915* (New York: Abrams, 1995); Alan Emmet, *So Fine a Prospect: Historic New England Gardens* (Hanover, N.H.: University Press of New England, 1996); Barbara Wells Sarudy, *Gardens and Gardening in the Chesapeake, 1700–1805* (Baltimore: Johns Hopkins University Press, 1998).

5. For the sake of simplicity and consistency, Martha Brookes Brown Hutcheson is referred to throughout this essay as "Hutcheson," although much of her professional practice was carried out under her maiden name, Martha Brookes Brown.

6. Biographical information has been compiled from ASLA membership application forms, letters, and other documents in MBHA. Hutcheson herself supplied brief biographical data for Clarence Fowler's "Three Women in Landscape Architecture [Beatrix Jones Farrand, Martha

Brookes Hutcheson, Marian Cruger Coffin]," *Cambridge School of Domestic and Landscape Architecture Alumnae Bulletin* 4 (April 1932): 7–12. The only other known previously published works on Hutcheson are Elizabeth Meade, "Martha Brookes Hutcheson, 1872 [*sic*]–1959: A Biographical Minute," *Landscape Architecture* 50 (Spring 1960): 181–82; Denise D. Royle, "Martha Brookes Hutcheson and Her Garden at Bamboo Brook" (undergraduate honors thesis in Landscape Architecture, Rutgers University, 1990), esp. 10–27, published in revised form as Denise Royle and Jean Marie Hartman, "Martha Brookes Hutcheson and Her Influence on the American Landscape," *Council of Educators in Landscape Architecture Selected Papers* 3 (August 1991): 153. Fuller discussions of Hutcheson's life and work are in Rebecca Warren Davidson, "Images and Ideas of the Italian Garden in American Landscape Architecture" (Ph.D. diss., Cornell University, 1994), esp. 322–78; idem, "*The Spirit of the* American *Garden*: Landscape and Cultural Expression in the Work of Martha Brookes Hutcheson," *Journal of the New England Garden History Society* 4 (Spring 1996): 22–29.

7. According to the *Art School Directory*, vol. 1 (Washington, D.C.: American Federation of the Arts, 1939), 79, the New York School of Applied Design for Women was founded shortly before Hutcheson enrolled, having been incorporated in 1892 as a charter member of the Federation, and offering instruction in "textile design, interior architecture, fashion illustration, commercial art and posters, [and] historic ornament." In spite of notable achievements made by women in the fine arts by the late nineteenth century, the written evidence makes clear that they were not generally expected to excel as painters or sculptors: "China painting and decorative art in general are the specialty of woman, who excels in the minor, personal artistic impulses and in this way gives vent to her restricted life," wrote E. A. Randall in "The Artistic Impulses in Men and Women," *Arena* 24 (October 1900): 420, quoted in Hill, *Grandmother's Garden*, 36.

8. A number of her original sketches and finished designs are preserved in her former home, Merchiston Farm, near Gladstone, New Jersey, now administered as the Bamboo Brook Outdoor Education Center by the Morris County Park Commission, to whom the property and Hutcheson's papers were bequeathed by her daughter and son-in-law in 1972.

9. Rhoda Holmes Nicholls (1854–1930) was born in Coventry and studied at London's Bloomsbury School of Art. She exhibited her work widely after coming to the United States in 1884, and won a number of awards, including a medal at the 1893 World's Columbian Exposition in Chicago. For further information, see the entry in *North American Women Artists of the Twentieth Century, A Biographical Dictionary*, ed. Jules Heller and Nancy G. Heller (New York: Garland, 1995), 406.

10. Only under wartime duress in 1942 did Harvard open its doors to women.

11. Marian Cruger Coffin, quoted in Fowler, "Three Women," 11–12. Coffin received her degree in landscape architecture from MIT in 1904 and went on to a remarkably successful career. She became the second woman to be made a Fellow of the American Society of Landscape Architects (the first was founding member Beatrix Jones Farrand), and is probably best known today for her work with Henry Francis Du Pont in creating the gardens at Winterthur. For more on Coffin, see Valencia Libby, "Marian Cruger Coffin: Landscape Architect of Distinction," *Preservation League of New York State Newsletter* 16 (Fall 1990): 4–5, and Nancy Fleming, *Money, Manure, and Maintenance: Ingredients for Successful Gardens of Marian Coffin, Pioneer Landscape Architect, 1876–1957* (Weston, Mass.: Country Place Books, 1995).

12. For more information on landscape architecture education for women in this era, see Dorothy May Anderson, *Women, Design, and the Cambridge School* (West Lafayette, Ind.: PDA Publishers, 1980); Jane Alison Knight, *An Examination of the History of the Lowthorpe School of Landscape*

Architecture for Women, Groton, Massachusetts (M.L.A. thesis, Cornell University, 1986); and the summary in Cynthia Zaitzevsky, "Education and Landscape Architecture," in *Architectural Education and Boston*, ed. Margaret Henderson Floyd (Boston: Boston Architectural Center, 1989), 20–34.

13. Hutcheson, quoted in Fowler, "Three Women," 9. It is interesting to note that this remembrance was published in a newsletter for alumnae of the Cambridge School, where perhaps it served as both justification and inspiration for other women to choose a career in landscape architecture.

14. For more on this notion, see Hill, *Grandmother's Garden*, esp. 143–46.

15. Guy Lowell, ed., *American Gardens* (Boston: Bates & Guild, 1902).

16. For more on Lowell, see Davidson, "Images and Ideas," 176–306. His architectural work has been documented by Douglas Howard Bonnell, "Boston Beaux–Arts: The Architecture of Guy Lowell with a Documentary Catalogue of His Works" (M.A. thesis, Tufts University, 1980).

17. "Option 3. Landscape Architecture," Massachusetts Institute of Technology, Boston, Department of Architecture [course catalog] (Boston, 1901), 75.

18. Hutcheson, quoted in Fowler, "Three Women," 10.

19. There is evidence that Hutcheson may have had a difficult relationship with Guy Lowell, whom she termed "jealous of women," among other things, in a handwritten note found in the margins of her copy of Mary Bronson Hartt, "Woman and the Art of Landscape Gardening," *The Outlook*, 28 March 1908, 695–704, in which Lowell is quoted as saying, "A woman will *fuss* with a garden in a way that no man will ever have the patience to do."

20. Coffin, quoted in Fowler, "Three Women," 12. Such prejudice continued unabated into the 1920s, even after women landscape architects had fully established themselves professionally. To cite just one example, in an article generally favorable toward coeducation in the field published in "School News," *Landscape Architecture* 13 (October 1922): 72–73, the Report of the Committee on Coeducation from the Second National Conference on Instruction in Landscape Architecture stated that "by receiving her professional training in contact with men, a woman has the advantage of learning her place sooner than she otherwise would. . . . It might even be suggested that a study of stenography would be especially useful for women in helping them to work in an office."

21. One instance of her professional struggles is evidenced in a letter from Frederick Law Olmsted Jr. apparently written in response to a plea from Hutcheson for help in a dispute she was having with a client over her fee. (Olmsted declined to become involved, stating, "I prefer not to go into such a matter except in a purely impartial judicial way and at the request of both parties to the disagreement."). FLO Jr. to Martha Brookes Brown, 15 March 1909.

22. Martha Brookes Brown, "The Garden Spirit," *The Cosmopolitan* 30 (April 1901): 579–88.

23. [Martha Brookes Brown], "Landscape Gardening: A Conversation," *The Outlook*, 24 July 1909, 726–39.

24. Martha Brookes Hutcheson, "The Use of the Hedge"; "Water in the Planning of the Garden: Harnessing Its Many Contributions to Our Use"; "The Importance of Arbors in the Garden: Their Value as Shade as Well as in Composition," *The House Beautiful* 53 (March–May 1923): 229–32; 360–62; 484–86.

25. Hutcheson was mentioned, for example, in "School News," *Landscape Architecture* 18 (April 1928): 249, where it was reported that "the high water mark of the [winter] term [at Lowthorpe] . . . has been three days of intensive criticism of assigned problems by Mrs. Martha Brookes Hutcheson of New York."

26. Hutcheson's attempt to restructure the Garden Club to make it more than, in her words, "a mere social gathering and mutual admiration party" (Hutcheson to Mrs. Linus H. Hall, 19 March 1931, MBHA) is a topic unto itself. Not surprisingly, many GCA members resented and resisted Hutcheson's often bluntly stated suggestions for changes and improvements in the group, but this did not stop her from continuing to address the subject. For more of her published thoughts on how the Garden Club could be a stronger political and civic force, see Martha Brookes Hutcheson, "Are Our Garden Clubs to Progress in Unison or Die of the Inertia of the Commonplace?" *Garden Club of America Bulletin*, 3d ser., no. 4 (July 1925): 21–24; idem, "The First Quarter Century of the Garden Club of America as Seen by an Old Member," *Garden Club of America Bulletin*, 6th ser., no. 7 (January 1938): 22–31. In the latter article she explains the "Wider Program" for Garden Clubs she had proposed in 1919, in order to "lessen the waste one finds today in the unprogressive, haphazard, individual garden clubs' yearly programs."

27. Marian Cruger Coffin, *Trees and Shrubs for Landscape Effects* (New York: Charles Scribner's Sons, 1940); Elsa Rehmann, *Garden-Making* (Boston: Houghton Milfflin, 1926).

28. Martha Brookes Hutcheson, "One of Our National Blights," *Garden Club of America Bulletin*, 3d ser., no. 12 (November 1926): 31. "Almost without exception, wherever our citizens, rich or poor, 'improve' our land by building on it, devastation is the accepted code of embellishment. First of all every trace of natural beauty in shrub growth must be eradicated,—grubbed out and burned, — and then this spot of lost opportunity, which can never again be brought back, must be decorated with foreign importations and a lawn." It is noteworthy that Hutcheson raised the issue of whether the perfect green lawn was either aesthetically or ecologically advisable at a time when most other designers would not even have thought of questioning its wholesale adoption in America. Strangely, Virginia Scott Jenkins, in an otherwise well-researched book, seems to have quite mis-represented Hutcheson's position on this issue. In *The Lawn: A History of an American Obsession* (Washington, D.C.: Smithsonian Institution Press, 1994), Jenkins accuses Hutcheson of "promoting the aesthetic ideal of the front lawn" (41 n. 31) when, in fact, to my knowledge, she always spoke out against it. For Hutcheson's strongest statement against the lawn as a home landscaping necessity, see her "Possible Inspiration through Garden Clubs toward Wiser and More Beautiful Plantings," *Garden Club of America Bulletin*, 4th ser., no. 16 (July 1931): 118.

29. Hutcheson, "Possible Inspiration," 118.

30. O. C. Simonds, *Landscape-Gardening* (New York: Macmillan, 1920; reprint, Amherst: University of Massachusetts Press / Library of American Landscape History, 2000). For a summary of the literature on the use of native plants in American landscape design by Simonds, Jensen, and others, see Robert E. Grese, *Jens Jensen: Maker of Natural Parks and Gardens* (Baltimore: Johns Hopkins University Press, 1992), esp. 52–61.

31. Edith A. Roberts and Elsa Rehmann, *American Plants for American Gardens* (New York: Macmillan, 1929), 8. Rehmann had included two photographs of Hutcheson's work in her earlier book, *Garden-Making*.

32. She apologizes in the foreword for the preponderance of her own designs: "They have not been chosen because they are superior in any way as examples of points to be emphasized, but because they form an available collection of personally taken detail, which it would be impossible to procure in any other way."

33. Martha Brookes Hutcheson, *The Spirit of the Garden* (Boston: Atlantic Monthly Press, 1923); hereafter cited by page number in the text.

34. For a more extensive discussion of Hutcheson's contribution in this regard, and the importance of the Italian model in American landscape design, see Davidson, "Images and Ideas."

35. It is particularly fortunate that Hutcheson included these three plans in the book. Although the MBHA and other sources have yielded one or two others, the great majority of her designs remain thus far undocumented by plans or other drawings.

36. The architect Herbert D. Hale designed the house at Undercliff.

37. Undercliff was one of the few Hutcheson designs that ever received a full and appreciative article in a national publication. See "The Garden of the Home of Dr. J. Henry Lancashire, Manchester, Mass., Mrs. Wm. A. Hutcheson, Landscape Architect," *House and Garden* 37 (June 1920): 42–43.

38. As she later described: "In 1902 I was called upon to locate and plan a garden for Mr. Frederick S. Moseley, the only stipulated requirement being that I should make the garden a part of an approach to the already established greenhouses and fruit and vegetable gardens." Martha Brookes Hutcheson, "Report of Work Done on Estate of Frederick S. Moseley, Esq., Newburyport, Massachusetts," typescript draft of documentation submitted to the Secretary of the Examining Board, American Society of Landscape Architects, 12 May 1920, in support of her application for membership, MBHA.

39. Ibid.

40. William Lawrence Bottomley, review of *The Spirit of the Garden* by Martha Brookes Hutcheson, *Architectural Record* 55 (February 1924): 205. Bottomley (1888–1951), a well-known country house architect of the period, worked with Hutcheson on alterations to Merchiston Farm made in 1927, according to a note in the MBHA.

41. [Leila Mechlin], "*The Spirit of the Garden*: A Review," *American Magazine of Art* 15 (January 1924): 731.

42. "What Gardens Are For," *New York Herald Tribune*, 13 November 1927, 22. The original price was $8.50; the reprint cost $3.50.

43. Edith V. R. Heard, "Departments: Garden Literature," *Garden Club of America Bulletin*, 3d ser., no. 18 (November 1927): 53.

44. Fletcher Steele, *Design in the Little Garden* (Boston: Atlantic Monthly Press, 1924), 36. Steele's book was part of the very popular Little Garden Series edited by Louisa Yeomans King.

45. Frank A. Waugh, *Formal Design in Landscape Architecture, A Statement of Principles with Special Reference to Their Present Use in America* (New York: Orange Judd, 1927), 49–51.

The Spirit of the
GARDEN

EGJ.

A SECLUDED CORNER IN THE GARDEN OF THE VILLA D'ESTE

THE SPIRIT
of the
GARDEN
by

MARTHA BROOKES HVTCHESON

WITH AN INTRODVCTION BY
ERNEST PEIXOTTO

Illustrated with Photographs

BOSTON
THE ATLANTIC MONTHLY PRESS

PRINTED IN THE UNITED STATES OF AMERICA

TO THOSE
WITH A PROGRESSIVE SPIRIT IN THEIR CONCERN FOR THE
FINE ART OF GARDEN MAKING
AND TO MY
LITTLE DAUGHTER
WHO HAS ITS JOYS STILL TO DISCOVER
THIS BOOK IS
DEDICATED

INTRODUCTION

It indeed gives me pleasure to write a short note of introduction to this admirable book by Martha Brookes Hutcheson, Member of the American Society of Landscape Architects, — who will perhaps be better known in the field of landscape gardening under her maiden name of Martha Brookes Brown, — though such a note seems quite unnecessary in the face of her own excellent foreword. The pictures, too, which have been used among those in illustration of the well-known gardens that she has designed speak for themselves of her competence to write and to think of garden design, and sufficiently introduce her to her readers.

Nevertheless, I feel that I should especially like to say a word in praise of the restrained tone and the sober spirit of her text, so free from the exuberances of many garden-books whose preoccupations seem to be, above all else, for color combinations, the massing of flowering shrubs, and the "picturesque features" and other excesses adored by horticultural gardeners.

The author of this book, on the contrary, goes back to those basic principles that underlie all true garden-making, the skeleton or bony structure upon which this art depends and which should be the first consideration in laying out a garden: its relation to the house; the adaptation of its plan to the conformation of its site; the due consideration of its various axes; the contrast of its gay flowers with the walls and hedges of green that should surround them and set them off, even as the painter contrasts the vivid color in his picture with the more sombre tones of the background.

And this simile holds doubly true; for, in large measure, the art of landscape-gardening forms a part of and is closely allied to the other plastic arts. Has not sculpture always been used to enhance the beauty of gardens and people their fountains and bosky glades with nymphs and dryads? Do not the gardener's shears shape and trim both tree and hedge to fit the forms created by the master's mind? Are not the yew-tree and the cedar, the cypress and the box modeled and clipped to fit their architectural surroundings, even as the decorative sculptor fits his figure into a pediment or into scale with a balustrade or cornice? And the tie of the gardener's art to architecture is too obvious even to be mentioned.

It was thoroughly understood by the men who laid out our earlier American gardens that were patterned after the "gardens of intelligence" planned in France and England by Lenôtre and his followers. Samuel Vaughan's regular plans for the grounds of Mount Vernon with their walled enclosures and box-patterned beds, the gardens of the James River estates and of the homes about Charleston, all bear witness to this fact.

But unfortunately, these cardinal principles of gardening were quite lost sight of at a later period when our gardeners were more concerned with mid-Victorian ideas of naturalistic effects, containing so-called picturesque features that bore no relation whatever to the house to which they were attached nor to their own surroundings. And it is only recently that a small group of landscape gardeners, worthy of the name, has brought back our thoughts to a real consideration of design as applied to the art of garden-planning.

To this group Martha Brookes Hutcheson belongs. Therefore I think that her book will be a most useful addition to garden literature and a helpful acquisition to the lover of gardens, both amateur and professional, and I predict that it will exert a real influence in the betterment of the art of landscape-gardening in America. For in it are embodied the true principles of garden design, as well as the proper uses of the green world controlled by the T square — all of which should give food for thought to anyone who is contemplating the making of a garden.

ERNEST PEIXOTTO.

FOREWORD

GARDEN books exist in great numbers which give comprehensive and helpful planting-charts, color-schemes and lists of valuable varieties of plants. There is a deeper need in the larger conception of the underlying principles of comprehensive planning, and I have found, time and again, that this broader view-point has been earnestly looked for by many amateurs, to whom the fact is very clear that all the planting material in the world is of little value if a sense of such basic principles as may be realized by all is lacking.

To take, for example, a planting which is needed in cutting across the end of a building where foreground planting is important: it makes little difference whether a dogwood, a tupelo, or a much despised ailanthus is used — the paramount consideration is the particular outline which the selected tree will ultimately produce, and the rarity of the plant is of secondary consideration. For another example we may take the importance of the massing of color and heights in a garden, which must be judged in their proper relation to each other as they affect the garden as a unit, the exact varieties of flowers or shrubs being — again — of secondary importance.

The keener insight becomes in the tastes and perceptions of property-owners in general, the greater will be the understanding of the need for fine planning, the realization of which is as yet very new in this country. An increasing ambition for gardens and the development of private places is growing apace, and with the undaunted energy and ease of adaptation in the American temperament, it is not difficult to predict the dawn of a far-seeing appreciation of all phases of the " great outdoors " such as has never existed. As a nation, we are just awakening to our wealth and our need for the conservation of our vast natural beauty with its amazing variety in scene and in plant life; and as individuals, we are slowly becoming conscious of the value of cultivated and æsthetic knowledge in adapting to our home surroundings the good principles in planning which have been handed down to us from the Old World. The more we know, the more we will make use of the great variety in growth already ours, — now commonly ignored, — which might lend itself so wonderfully to our crying needs. It is all at our very door. Gradually the wider vision will grow more and more general, and in its expression we shall be known, in years to come, not only as a nation of great acquisition but of great perception in our standard of this art.

Having retired from years of active practice in the making of gardens, I take this opportunity of outlining some of the principles which I have found are not generally understood in their true importance. I have been conscious for years of an ever-widening group of men and women who are quite alive to a finer standard in planting and who have an increasing desire for better gardens. This small minority are not yet satisfied with their accomplishments, and this very quality of dissatisfaction and the vision for a broader achievement mark them as apart from the general average or majority, who in their contented satisfaction, " know not that they know not."

The technicalities which can only be known through professional training and experience are by no means dealt with in this book, its topics being only sufficiently touched upon to arouse interest and insight in a broad conception of the creation and reason for various arrangements. The broader and more general this conception becomes, the greater will be the advance in our standard of fine gardens and general plantings.

If in these pages some points are made which seem to ignore or belittle the many individual triumphs in gardens which now exist, I can only beg of those owners to recognize their membership in a small minority, through whose leadership a better general standard will be formed. Every example of good planning and true beauty which exists today will go far toward establishing a greater knowledge in the achievements of tomorrow.

A word of explanation is necessary in defense of the use of so many illustrations made from places or gardens for which I have been wholly or in part responsible as the landscape architect. They have not been chosen because they are superior in any way as examples of points to be emphasized, but because they form an available collection of personally taken detail, which it would be impossible to procure in any other way. Their present use has been permitted through the courtesy of the owners, for which sincere gratitude is here expressed. I also want to take this opportunity to record my appreciation of the unfailing loyalty and encouragement of the many friends and clients who through their unchanging interest made the years fly by on wings of happy purpose and enabled the joy of "dreaming true."

Martha Brookes Hutcheson.

A LIST OF PLACES
MADE WHOLLY OR IN PART BY THE AUTHOR
AND ILLUSTRATED IN THE BOOK

Undercliff	The late CHARLES HEAD (Present owner, DR. JAMES H. LANCASHIRE)	*Manchester, Mass.*
Crowhurst	FRANCIS M. WHITEHOUSE, ESQ.	*Manchester, Mass.*
Maudesleigh	FREDERICK S. MOSELEY, ESQ.	*Newburyport, Mass.*
Headlands	The late CHARLES HEAD	*Westport, New York*
Sosiego	The late MRS. DANIEL LORD	*Lawrence, Long Island*
Whitegates Farm	MRS. HENRY MARQUAND	*Bedford Hills, New York*
Craigie House	MISS LONGFELLOW	*Cambridge, Mass.*
Welwyn	MRS. HAROLD I. PRATT	*Glen Cove, Long Island*
Highwall	MRS. OLIVER AMES	*Prides Crossing, Mass.*
Indian Neck	The late STEPHEN M. WELD	*Wareham, Mass.*
Merchiston Farm	WILLIAM A. HUTCHESON, ESQ.	*Gladstone, New Jersey*
Poplar Hill	FREDERICK B. PRATT, ESQ.	*Glen Cove, Long Island*
Oldfields	MRS. ROBERT BACON	*Westbury, Long Island*
Brick House	ANDREW V. STOUT, ESQ.	*Red Bank, New Jersey*

CONTENTS

ILLUSTRATIONS

ILLUSTRATIONS

The
FLOWER
Garden

I

THE FLOWER GARDEN

GARDENS are favorite spots the world over. The innate sense of man for generations has evidently craved some concentrated spot for the blending of all that goes to make up the beauty of the outdoor world in color, form, light, perfume; the play of the seasons; the sound and sight of the birds and insect life; the opportunity for the intelligent and loving touch that the human being can lend to the arrangement of nature; the ceaseless play of imagination and realization of achievement and the centred interest in the home — where these meet together in the ever-changing beauty of our gardens. The larkspur is incomplete without the humming bird, the rose without the dew; the evening primrose courts the twilight; the subtle form of arrangement plays with the mystery of flower-form and outline; and with this blending of those things which we all seek and love we find a peace in our gardens which other places seldom give. The garden is not only the exquisite playground of the home, but the resting-place of the spirit — the place of inspiration and promise, of tranquillity and intense personal claim, and we are held and inspired by it.

To those who know this it is needless to say a word, for the garden spirit is in them, and all who possess it know it to be one of their greatest treasures. It has lived on and on for centuries and may well be counted as among the most civilized of our senses. The very history of ornament has sprung from the flowers themselves; for long before the origin of the lotus motif, which is the basis for so much Egyptian design, there must have been a keen love of the lotus. The acanthus leaf impressed its beauty on the eye and heart of man for generations before it was forever immortalized in the classic Corinthian capital. The cherry blossom, which one finds underlying so much in Chinese formal ornament and insignia, was but the offspring of the appeal of the exquisite form of that springtime bloom. One finds all these proofs of the intense relation between flowers and the human being long before the Christian era, and our growing interest in gardens at the present day is not surprising when such great variety in plants and ease of achievement, through transportation, have never before been known.

Early in 1500 Sir Thomas More said: "They set great store by their gardens. In them they have vineyards, all manner of fruit, herbs and flowers, so pleasant, so well furnished, and so fynely kepte that I never saw thynge more fruiteful, nor better trimmed in any place. Their studie and diligence herein commeth not onely of pleasure but also of a certain strife and contention that is between strete and strete, concerning the trimmings, husbanding and furnishing of their gardens, everye man for his owne parte. And verelye you shall not lightelye finde in all the citie anyethinge that is more commodies eyther for the profite of the citizens or for pleasure."

Madame de Sévigné wrote in 1671: "I do not know what you have been doing this morning; for my part, I have been in the dew up to my knees, laying lindens. I am making winding alleys all around my park which will be of great beauty. If my son loves woods and walks he will be sure to bless my memory."

So the love for the outdoor effect is no new fad, no interest which has sprung up in our minds of late. From the earliest times there were gardens, and the world is the better to-day for the touch of gentleness and calm they have given to all who knew them.

Again, at a nearer date, in a letter from Matthew Arnold to his daughter we find this delightful touch of the enthusiasm of autumn work: "You can imagine the relief with which I have been going about the garden this morning and planting. Numbers of summer flowers are still blooming. The birds are happy in the open weather, and the sweet robins keep following Collis and me about as we open the ground and plant rhododendrons." We may be sure he enjoyed the bloom of those plants a few years later with far more interest than he would have felt had Collis had the entire care.

So let us all have gardens, for we shall be but following in the footsteps of those of past ages, and but expressing the love of the garden that has been in our hearts for generations. Above all, let us have a sense of seclusion in our flowered space, that the calm and peace shall in no way be broken. Here belong the song of birds and the hum of insects. When solitude is looked for, the garden is the place to which we naturally turn. Let it have cool, shaded places, where out of the summer sun one may steal to sit, and, with the sound of dripping water near by, see the brilliant flower-beds in their masses of gorgeous color standing out in the full sunlight, with the bees at work among them and the blue sky overhead. And let the garden be just near enough to the house to be part of the life of its inmates where they may go without effort, in the day or the evening. Does everyone know the garden in the half evening light, when all sharp outline is blended into one luxuriant composition of flower forms, paths, and fountain, held in a mass of green that is unlike that of day? And do we all know it by moonlight, when all green is gone and distant corners are lost in darkness, while perhaps a white evening-primrose opens its bloom to the summer night and stands pale and cool with the moon's rays upon it, and its long shadow cast across the pathway? It is at these moments that our gardens are of unspeakable worth to us and we begrudge no care that has gone to their making.

I remember a little garden in Normandy about the home of an old Frenchwoman, which gave me the feeling that it was the real setting of this little woman's life. On high plaster walls, which made a perfect background for the flowering elder outside, the peach trees were carefully trained, their tiny green fruit the smallest kind of promise of the mellow peaches yet to come; the rose bushes, in the true French way, were clipped up the length of the stem and left to burst forth in all their unchecked beauty at the tops of the plants. At regular intervals these bordered the path — with low flowers growing in profusion under them — as a boundary to her regularly planted vegetable garden, which we found was her means of support. It was full of the light green leaves of lettuce and tall splendid round onion blossoms with their long stems holding them well in air; and near by the bright radishes she had been tying in bunches for the market lent a decorative bit of usefulness to the quiet place. She was a perfectly happy self-supporting peasant woman, and I have never forgotten her look of delight as we admired her flowers and fruit. She bustled about in white cap and sabots, with a radiant smile, making us taste her lettuce and peas, and we went away with large bunches of roses in our arms and the garden spirit in our hearts.

These little humble places abound in France and in England, too, where the love of the garden is keenly felt. At times we find their counterpart here in America, but much too seldom, for the nurseryman's example of disconnected groups of miscellaneous shrubs has for years been taking the place of true garden-making, and the simple flowering space, such a valuable part of the little home, seems often forgotten.

In Massachusetts there is a garden which is so old and has had its own way for so long, that it has broken through its original bounds by the river and has wandered back into the orchard on one side and into the vegetable garden on the other, and so through its truancy lends the gayety of poppies to the melon patch and of morning-glories to the bean poles; and, to make the most of its independence and frolic, some campanulas find sheltered spots about the old apple-trees. But this flower garden can afford to have enough for itself and to spare, for at all seasons, from April to November, a wealth of color is found here. It is one of those places in which painters delight, with its masses of bloom — with wonderful highlights upon them — where everything is growing in healthy abundance, with just enough haphazard self-sowing, and still not in uncomfortable confusion. Here in the autumn, when the touch of the night frost is beginning to change the colors on all sides, one may sit in the warm corner of the grape-covered wall with the asters and chrysanthemums still holding their bloom and the barberries growing redder day by day. Those October days! When every blossom is doubly dear, — for it is of the last, — when late pansies and sweet alyssum bloom in spite of frost, and when the long summer is all but gone, we begrudge each hour as it slips away, and agree with him who wrote: —

> The daughters of the year one by one
> Through this still garden pass, dance into light
> And die into the shade.

To those last days we owe a thought in the planning of the garden, that there may be some bloom here and there as long as possible in the spot which has been full of color for so many months.

To study the gardens of different periods, which were naturally affected by the fashions of their day, is not only interesting but instructive in many ways, for from them valuable principles are learned, and many of these may be applied to our more modern needs. The formality, for example, which is found in the old villa-gardens outside of Rome and on the Tuscan hills is of great interest, more for the lines on which they were originally laid out than for the flowers they may have contained. Many of them were planted so long ago that they are now but ghosts of their original plan, and the old stone-work is covered with moss that softens every surface. In these places one comes unexpectedly upon a glimpse of the blue sky overhead, reflected perhaps in some long basin of water at one's feet, in which surrounding trees also are pictured, and the whole framed in a wealth of blue myosotis, growing luxuriantly in every crack and crevice of the fine old water-basin and glistening with the mist of spray upon it in the noonday sun. And again we may find some green bosket far off at one corner, so inviting a spot, apart in its shade and tranquillity, that to linger there is one's impulse; and yet to be again in quest of new discoveries, new treasures to be found, is one's only reason for leaving. Here, about these old villas, are spots of seclusion, of quiet, of beauty, so near and so personal that one can never tire of them, never cease to wish to go back again and again; and if that may never be, the thought of them lives in our minds, and we are unsatisfied until we have created in our own land some other spot which at least breathes forth some of their satisfying expression, even if it has not their advantages of great age and tradition as a setting. The Italians apparently knew well the value of a shaded place lying in close proximity to one full of sunlight, each being related to the other in plan. In many villas the space about the house itself is entirely in the open, but beyond the gardens and forecourts a wooded spot is invariably introduced

8

at an inviting distance, generally covering a considerable area, with walks laid out formally between the trees, where it is a relief to wander out of the sun and heat, and yet a pleasure to come back to the flowering space where all is brilliant and intricate in its upkeep.

The elements to be considered in the planning of a flower garden are so many and so complex that it is a difficult task to outline the most important ones, and yet it is essential that some general principles should be understood; for through their insight, owners have in their control the opportunity for much more personal and beautiful gardens than are generally found to-day.

By taking up a few points in garden-construction it will be of value to see how most of the principles prove that the possibility of interesting garden-making lies in the hands of everyone who can grasp the vision of logical composition and fitness as they contribute to the æsthetic whole.

First of all, the size and type of a garden are of great consequence in its relation, not only to the style of the house, but to its importance as a dwelling. An elaborate house, for instance, surrounded by a parterre over which one should pass before reaching the garden, at once creates — in its effect architecturally — the very note of formality which is needed. This treatment belongs to the general scheme of the house, and through its expanse and formality prevents the house from having the least suggestion of the cottage type. The garden, under these conditions, may be large and varied in the architectural features embodied in it. Intricate water-schemes, walls, peristyles, and loggias all belong here, as well as wall fountains and espalier fruits and bay trees, and its vastness and perfection of detail will lend so finished a note that the limit of the house will seem to be reached only at the extreme end of the garden.

On the other hand, in the more intimate form of home where the architecture suggests nothing of formality, we cannot bring the garden close enough. Whether it is laid out formally or informally, a simple garden near the house may creep up and look in at the very windows. Its accessibility in this case is a part of this house, and its closeness the expression of personal care and interest.

The first formal lay-out has been borrowed in idea and sentiment from important places, the second from the simpler homes, of the Old World. It rests with individual owners to decide which they will emulate; but whichever type is followed, the opportunity for the placing and treatment of the garden is of equal importance. In either case it must be made to look as if it had grown there in perfect relation to all about it.

The second important detail in any garden is the main line of approach which connects it with the house. This main axis should lead up to some important point of a house, and in their relation one to the other the garden and the house should form a unit. To take advantage of every line of axis one can — if a garden lies in formal relation to the house — is to make the most of opportunity. In this way the vantage points of one's garden are brought into the very make-up of the house itself when the garden is seen from within the house, and vice versa. When you enter your formal garden from its farthest gateway, your eye is led by the composition of green in bay trees or cedars or hedge-lines and pathways to the formal trees on either side of the opposite entrance, and again, on the same line, through it to the architectural columns each side of the doorway, and so to the very door itself. You have harnessed the scheme of the house to that of the garden, and by doing so have increased the charm of both and given a consistent reason to the whole affair.

If you lead to an unimportant point in your house, the garden will

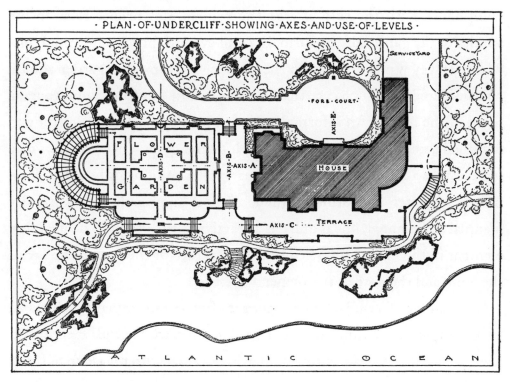

· PLAN · OF · UNDERCLIFF · SHOWING · AXES · AND · USE · OF · LEVELS ·

never suggest any relation to the home; the fact that the real "anat-
omies," so to speak, of the house and the garden do not hang together
will create a note of discord. I have seen a garden of no small upkeep,
which actually led to a pantry window, and another which led to the
abrupt corner of the house. It seems past belief that such lack of vision
and sense of the rudiments of composition could be possible, but we
find examples of this kind of lack of relation in surprising instances as
soon as we look for them. They exist by the hundreds, and their owners
are generally quite oblivious to them. It seems almost unkind to disturb
such unobservant peace of mind by pointing out these mistakes, for
when one does, the fault generally looms up in such distressing evidence
that the alterations on the house or garden are planned for within the
next twenty-four hours!

While formal gardens, when properly treated, are always made in compliance with the rule of axis, the principle of proper relationship applies to the garden of less formality and even to the very informal one. The pathway which leads from the house to the rambling garden should be considered with such care that it seems to flow out from some vantage point of the house. An informal path can lead up with so beautiful and dignified a curve to the steps of a porch or the grape-covered arbor of a terrace that its importance is quite as great as the straight scheme on which we enter the formal garden. If both approaches are carefully planned and planted, one is quite as attractive as the other. The deciding element in the choice lies with the architecture of the house, the lay of the land, and the taste of the owner.

Illustrations of a well-planned spot are often less illuminating than bad examples; so let us think of small gardens that we have all seen which have been laid out on a portion of an existing lawn with regard to nothing which apparently joined them to anything else. They suggest the same relation to the house that a gay rug might if one placed it at random out upon the greensward. We have seen rectangular patches like this placed directly between the house and a wonderful distant view, which should have had as its foreground so simple a treatment that nothing could prevent the eye from taking in, as one unbroken stretch, the space between one's very foothold and the distant horizon line; and yet we find all too frequently a rectangular patch called a garden, — sometimes small, sometimes of great extent, — deliberately placed with regard to nothing but itself, with no connecting relation to the house, with no regard to the country about it, an utter blot on the face of the earth, a stamp of the lack of feeling and perception on the owner's part, a meaningless spot which is a bad example to everyone who sees it — except to him who has the eyes to see in it a good example of a bad thing.

Then comes the third important detail, in the opportunity of going from scheme to scheme. For example : suppose one has a fine wood, not very far off, which would make a delightful flanking for a formal garden on one end, yet this wood is just too far away from the house to make the garden extend from it to the house. One might feel a choice must be made in the garden between proximity to the wood and proximity to the house. Suppose the charm of the wood prevails : one cannot resist the temptation of making its deep shade come in close relation to the sunny brilliant space filled with flowers, and the decision is made to go toward the wood-line with the garden. It is not a bad choice ; but two technical obstacles have been run into which must be surmounted. First, one of the hardest, though most interesting, things to do is to create a beautiful transition between an edge of woodland and a garden adjoining it. Second, how can so thoroughly artificial a spot as a formal garden be introduced when no formality exists around it ? For formality must spring from formality.

An architectural note from which the garden-plan can spring must therefore be created. For that note, then, go back to the house and use some detail there as a starting-point ; create from this some simple though formal green-treatment, like a hedge-enclosed parterre of green turf, and from this — going through a gateway which conforms to the same house-detail as an axis, and working always toward the garden-site — go into another level of green, which might be made quite shady by vine-covered arbors surrounding a tranquil pool. From this, go through an orchard which is again planted to conform to the axes of the house and garden, and enter your garden here. In this way the two difficulties have been overcome in tying the garden by a succession of related approaches to the woods and the house ; and yet the garden is related to

13

its surroundings and no larger than necessary. By still further treatment the garden can be blended into the wood-margin by paths which continue into the cool green growth, following the formality in path-treatment or not, as the place suggests.

We seldom tie things together enough. Going from one enclosure or scheme, so to speak, to another — though each may be very simple — is much more interesting than the planting that is realized at a glance, and the combinations of arrangements to make things seem involved and mysterious are never-ending. Variety can be made within the actual garden by dividing it into different sections. The entrance, for instance, hedged off from an intermediate terrace-section, from which we look down into a central garden: from this we may pass through arches, and gates in low walls, and slight steps, to a rose garden, or the approach to a tennis court, or anything which gives the excuse for still another outdoor enclosure. The reasonable complexity of a garden makes it inviting.

And here we come to a fourth great detail, one that we can never afford to cease to search for or make excuses for: the natural rolling of land, which gives us the chance for limitless effects and uses through the change of levels. They are as important as any other feature through which we get variety and surprise.

Through the use of steps we not only solve practical problems toward making the impossible quite possible, but we add enormously to the picturesque in what we are creating, and find another opportunity for added composition. If the difference in grades is great enough we can have vine- or fruit-covered walls. Where would Italy be if her gardens were robbed of walls and steps? One can have little steps, four inches only in rise, with long stretches of path between; one can have groups of

14

steps with green shrub-plantings about them. Then there are the small masonry-steps, with their sides well covered by vines, and — in important, formal gardens — splendid flights of steps, with landings and balustrades; and these, when well treated, are as important as any part of a whole garden. Sometimes we have but the slightest fall in grade to work with, but one foot is better than nothing in the difference between a garden and the approach leading to it. This gives two shallow steps down, of six inches each, and with a slight wall in addition rising up, the effect of the garden becomes that of a place apart. You have changed your level of approach; you have gone down two slight steps — though they may be very broad — and you have entered another place. You are in the garden!

We do not stop to think of all this, but we unconsciously feel it. Isn't intimacy gained in this way? Alas, how many flowered places have but one level! How their entire story is told in one sentence. How limited are the backgrounds they furnish for scenes they might hold. How meagre are they in the attributes of a real garden!

For our fifth detail of importance, we now come to the green used in the construction of gardens. It is this that gives us our backgrounds, our contrasts, our proportions, our perspective — above all, our shadows.

All gardens need plenty of green with varying amounts of color. Most gardens have too solid a mass of color and too little well-planned green. The informal note in them may be the flowers in their airy growth and beauty of outline. The larger notes of shrubbery are what form the constructive garden-planting, and these should be under perfect control, whether they are clipped in shape or of an informal growth.

Too much green and few flowers is a better fault than too much bloom and little green. Many plantings are merely thick mats of flower-bloom

15

arrangement in geometrically planned flower-beds. The heights vary only with the flowers planted, and while they may reflect credit on the skill of the gardener in flower culture, they lack everything else. The owners have had the opportunity of making their gardens places of restfulness and pleasure to those looking for a picturesque and livable quality, but having been blind to possibilities, have merely produced a spectacle with which the uneducated eye only is pleased, because no sense is appealed to but the crude love of a massing of color.

If the same amount of labor had been guided, the importance of having the flowers offset by taller greens to emphasize their outline would not have been overlooked. The garden would have been approached with some taller growth of shrubs or even old trees for its foreground, and a really beautiful enclosure would have been made of it, full of the sense of graceful boughs overstretching the paths, or of deep recesses of black-green shadow making some of its pathways seem invitingly cool and secluded.

Small trees in gardens, like dogwood, magnolia, thorns, and laburnum, give but a short period of bloom; their importance lies in their giving foreground and outline and style and age, and they play an important part in the values of light and shade. The dense shadows of our gardens we get from green growth. The emphasis of our pathways we get from clipped margins of green turf or hedge, and from our bay trees which flank them. Our seats are given inviting seclusion by their background of green hedge. The tranquillity and dignified expanse of open spaces of greensward in our gardens we gain through our closely cut green turf.

Green is needed just as much as color, only it should always be kept well within bounds and control.

16

THE FLOWER GARDEN

And now we have established our garden with relation to the house, its approach through schemes of different treatments, its walls, and its steps and paths with various levels. It has clipped hedges and formal evergreens, interspersed with carefully placed notes of the small tree-growth, and with great trees standing about it and beyond it to make it look thoroughly established in its environment. There are comfortable shady seats, which are placed where we can hear and see the dripping fountain or reflections in the still round pool, and there are arbors to pass through, and bird baths, and a dial, and greensward leading to gateways and hedges.

When this is ready, to this creation is added that final gay and God-given expression of exquisite sprightliness and variety — the flowers! Their part is too subtly beautiful to try to describe. The whole setting of the garden has been created to receive them, and they come and go in their fleeting succession of bloom in this established setting, with a certainty and accuracy of beauty which is a miracle. They have arrived to enter into their parts and play them charmingly in the drama of the garden. The foxgloves in their season will fill a certain corner in their special place in proximity to the high box and taller lilies. The yellow roses and trumpet vine have their steps and walls to cling to, and columbines, when they grow in a half shady corner with some gray stone-work and yew or pearl-bush leaves near by, will not want to stop blooming when their part should end, that later flowers might occupy the stage.

So the flower garden, as our ideal of it expands and our need of it becomes more real, is a place to go to and stay in — not a place to observe and pass through, or a mere cutting-ground for bloom. It is a part of the house which, without the limit of roof or walls, is still encompassed by enlightened planning. In our opportunity for the blending together of the laws of architecture and of the plant world, and by using and knowing the secrets of both, we shall make more and more wonderful gardens. We do not want vastness and pomp alone; we want detail, and mystery, and variety; above all, we want surprise in our gardens. These are the elements which go to make the true garden-spirit, which really appeals to the human heart — and that is what gardens are for.

TAORMINA, SICILY

UNDERCLIFF

SHOWING USE OF LEVELS. SEE AXIS B, PAGE 11

UNDERCLIFF
SHOWING USE OF LEVELS. SEE AXIS C, PAGE 11

SOSIEGO

USE OF ITALIAN OIL JAR AS POINT IN LINE OF AXIS

UNDERCLIFF

FROM A SIDE PATH OF THE GARDEN. SEE PAGE 11

UNDERCLIFF

SHOWING APPROACH TO GARDEN. SEE AXIS C, PAGE 11

OLDFIELDS

A TERRACE ADJOINING THE GARDEN

OLDFIELDS

TEMPLE D'AMOUR SEEN OVER THE WATER BASIN THROUGH THE CENTRAL AXIS
OF THE GARDEN

OLDFIELDS
DETAIL OF TEMPLE D'AMOUR

MERCHISTON FARM

THREE PHOTOGRAPHS ILLUSTRATING THE POSSIBILITY OF BRINGING A BUILDING
DOWN TO GRADE IN EFFECT WHERE ALL OR PART OF THE FOUNDATION IS IN
EVIDENCE. THOUGH EIGHT FEET IN HEIGHT OF FOUNDATION ARE PLANTED OUT
WITH SHRUBS AT THE SOUTH END OF THE HOUSE, THE CENTRAL PORTION IS
BROUGHT INTO INTIMATE GRADE RELATION WITH THE ORCHARD LEVEL BY
THE INTRODUCTION OF BROAD ROUGH STONE STEPS AND TURF APPROACH
BETWEEN THEM. THE TWO NECESSARY RETAINING WALLS BOUNDING THEIR
SIDES ARE CONCEALED BY SHRUBS PLANTED IN MASSES IN THE NATURAL
GRADE

MERCHISTON FARM

A NEARER DETAIL OF THE PLANTING AND TREATMENT

SHOWING GRADE TO BE CONSIDERED

VILLA D'ESTE

MAIN AXIS THROUGH HEDGES, STEPS, AND TERRACES TO CENTRE OF PALACE,
WATER BEING INTRODUCED ON SEVERAL LEVELS

TAORMINA, SICILY

THE HEDGE IS OF LAVENDER, WITH LITTLE TUFTS LEFT AT REGULAR INTERVALS
FOR ORNAMENT AND FOR BLOOM

TAORMINA, SICILY

SMALL PRIVATE MODERN GARDEN

WELWYN

"A PLACE TO STAY IN — NOT TO PASS THROUGH . . . NOR MERELY A CUTTING-
GROUND FOR BLOOM"

WELWYN
ILLUSTRATING THE INTEREST GAINED BY GOING DOWN INTO A GARDEN

WELWYN

ILLUSTRATING THE EFFECT GAINED BY ONE FOOT IN GRADE BEING PLANNED
WITH TWO SLIGHT STEPS, OF SIX INCHES EACH IN RISE. SEE PAGE 14

WELWYN

DETAIL OF LOW PIERCED-BRICK GARDEN-WALL

HADDON HALL, ENGLAND
THE USE OF STEPS JOINING TWO TERRACES

WELWYN
AN INTIMATE SIDE-PATH IN THE GARDEN, ILLUSTRATING THE ADVANTAGE OF
A LAVISH USE OF GREEN IN ITS COMPOSITION

CROWHURST
A CORNER OF THE GARDEN WHERE IT JOINS THE WOODLAND

INFORMAL TREATMENT OF ROUGH STEPS, AMPLE WIDTH BEING
ALLOWED FOR THE OVERHANGING GROWTH OF SHRUBS OR VINES

CROWHURST

POSITION OF TERRACE GARDEN, ABOVE NATURAL WOODS BORDERING THE
MANCHESTER COAST

CROWHURST

APPROACH TO GARDEN FROM LEVEL BELOW IT

CROWHURST

THE GARDEN WHICH "CREEPS UP AND LOOKS IN AT THE VERY WINDOWS"

TWO DETAILS OF THE GARDEN AT CROWHURST

VILLA ROSAZZI, GENOA

DETAIL OF THE GREEN PATH WHICH CONNECTS SEVERAL LEVELS OF GARDENS

MARGINAL TREATMENT OF STEPS WHICH OBLITERATES ALL HARD LINES BY THE
USE OF OVERHANGING VINES

VILLA ROSAZZI, GENOA

WHERE A GREEN PATH WINDS UP AND DOWN A STEEP HILLSIDE, MAKING NUM-
BERLESS POSITIONS FOR ORNAMENT AND INTEREST. THIS TEMPLE D'AMOUR
COMMANDS A WONDERFUL VIEW OF THE SEA IN THE DISTANCE

POPLAR HILL

GARDEN STEPS, SHOWING MAINTENANCE OF PROPER VINE-GROWTH, NO
ARCHITECTURAL FEATURE BEING HIDDEN

POPLAR HILL

APPROACH TO GARDEN FROM ABOVE

POPLAR HILL

TAKING ADVANTAGE OF ABRUPT GRADE TO MAKE THE STEPS THE IMPORTANT
FEATURE OF A GARDEN

POPLAR HILL

DETAIL OF BALUSTRADE AND STEPS LEADING FROM UPPER
LEVEL TO THE FLOWER GARDEN

A GARDEN HOUSE NEAR FLORENCE

MAUDESLEIGH

THE DIAL

The
Importance
~of~
AXIS

II

THE IMPORTANCE OF AXIS

XIS in landscape design is the backbone of any planting plan which relates a garden or a pleasure ground to the house or to other parts of the formal outdoor planting. The importance of axis does not seem to be understood well enough by the average person. It is so vital in construction that the attention even of children should be so directed to good examples of its use in landscape design or architecture (and likewise to the missed opportunities), that at an early age the coming generation may be trained to see this underlying principle, without which the grandeur and symmetry of all great planting and architectural treatment here and in Europe will be unappreciated and only half seen. One finds masterly uses of axis at every turn in Europe. Striking examples of its importance are, for instance, found in the long vistas and consecutive treatment of plantings in Versailles, the Villa d'Este, in the lay-out of Paris, or at the Taj Mahal of India. Our national capital, Washington, might have been a more far-reaching example of fine axis-arrangement in this country if the plans of L'Enfant, the eminent landscape architect of George Washington's day, had been adhered to in full. L'Enfant was naturally influenced by Lenôtre's work and by the examples of fine planning in Europe.

The infringements which were constantly made in Washington upon the great plan of a Mall, in the placing of important buildings and open spaces in relation to each other, is of too common knowledge to need reference. The blind indifference to this fine art in the past hundred

47

and fifty years has left unchecked liberty for those who were ignorant of what went to the making of beautiful cities, and the L'Enfant plan for Washington was entirely disregarded until the Park Commission of 1901, appointed under the influence of Senator McMillan, started the heavy task of bringing the public as well as the Mall back into line. To-day the Commission of Fine Arts — the direct heir of the 1901 Commission — has the purpose in hand of preserving the Washington plan from further encroachments.

We may be proud of the fact that Washington is being protected from the vandalism of ignorance and greed, and we see appearing, as if by magic, consecutive and imposing treatments of axes which are based on the mighty and beautiful law of logical sequence between one point and another in the relation of architecture and planting.

The most recent achievement is the Lincoln Memorial, which has been placed in absolute relation to the dome of the Capitol and the Washington Monument, through a line of axis on which is established the great reflecting basin of water, flanked by a tree-bordered vista of great length and generous, masterly proportions. The exact centre of the dome lies in relation to the centre not only of the Lincoln Memorial, but of the basin and of the vista by which the two great national structures are connected. This logical tying together of the country's Capitol with the building which expresses the memory of Lincoln's great spirit is made very real to everyone who has the vision to see in it that magic line of axis which starts with the centre of a prominent building and ends far off in another all-important point of an equally prominent one.

The masterly handling of this principle — found all over the world where knowledge of planting in relation to architecture has had its place — holds our interest as no informality of treatment can ever do.

This quality of fascination is in no way dependent upon size alone. The same law of dignity and balance which holds in the Lincoln Memorial in Washington, or the Place de la Concorde in Paris underlies the relation through axis between a house and its garden or a street entrance, the intervening dooryard, and the house door. The proportions are different; but the mesmeric influence of balance in sequence and logical, picturesque arrangement is under the same great law. In creating formal places we build on the major axis or axes, and on definite minor axes which lie in relation to them, and like all great principles, we

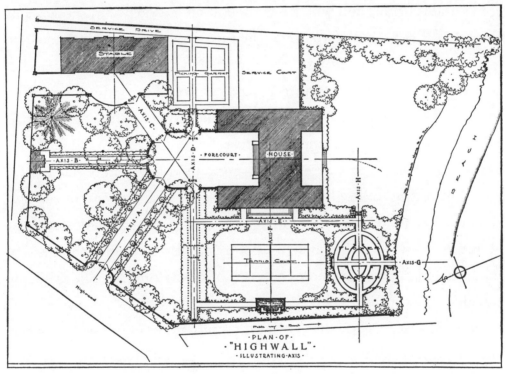

·PLAN·OF·
·"HIGHWALL"·
·ILLUSTRATING·AXIS·

find that their influence, in small ways as in great, is marked by unchanging truth and value. A picturesque arrangement out of doors is seldom successful unless the law of axis and balance is evident enough to make the superimposed informal detail enhanced by it. Far be it from me to give the impression that informality is to be done away with and that treatment of anything should be stereotyped and handcuffed in formality. The formal underlying construction should be more commonly understood as something on which to play with our informalities of beautiful, unexpected, green growth. Formality is by no means gaunt or bald. It can pierce green woods in paths, and add dignity and beauty to every upright tree-trunk or fern which borders them. It can use a distant mountain, by bringing it in relation to a terrace by a judicious clearing, and yet leave every tree-branch which frames the distance in balanced, exquisite outline. We have all seen slashes cut through woodland to gain an outlook, with no sense of the value of the middle ground or the ruthlessly destroyed intermediate growth as a frame or setting. The foreground coming in sharp relation to a distant view always makes it farther away in composition. The introduction of intermediate detail at one distant point, or at varied positions in perspective, draws out the scheme and makes the final picture — which is the objective point — not only more picturesque but far more interesting in its illusive distance. The arrangement of an axis should never be barren and unimaginative in the incidental treatment along its length, but the objective point and its relation to the starting point should not be interrupted. It is the maintaining of this principle which creates the line of axis.

In establishing this relation between plantings and buildings to the best advantage, too much emphasis cannot be given to the necessity of establishing collaboration between an architect and a landscape architect in the very first planning and placing of a house and its surroundings. There are parts of the house which essentially belong to the garden and parts of the garden which are as essentially parts of the house, and there is no separating them if a successful scheme of the whole is to be realized. For a landscape architect to add a garden or terrace treatment after an architect has finished the house is always to make the most of a patched-up undertaking, and the great axes and most valuable points in correlation are impossible to create at their best. The two minds should work together while the project is still on paper, each foreseeing in his own undertaking the fullest outcome of perfected detail, which calls distinctly for the two professions. For an architect to ignore this point and to establish the general scheme of outdoor arrangement in terraces, garden design, and so forth, trusting to a planting being made later by someone who is willing to fill out his half-accomplished work, is unfair to the owner, who too often never realizes how great an opportunity is lost. To the person who is to create the very composition of the planting should belong the creation of the original composition of the outdoor treatment. This coöperative planning of a successful undertaking may easily be looked upon as the overlapping or common ground of the two professions. The fact that so often this is overlooked, and an architect holds the whole undertaking in his hands up to the point where he must call in a nurseryman — who will do the planting according to his untrained suggestion — is due to ignorance of the public concerning what an architect should not undertake, and what they should look for in a landscape architect, if the fullest opportunity of any undertaking is to be seized. The door of a house opening upon a terrace, which again by a flight of steps drops to a garden, is a point of decision which belongs to two minds. The door and steps and their planting are just as much a part of the garden as of the house, and the original decision should be made simultaneously in the treatment of the entire scheme. The cedars and distance through a gateway lying beyond the flowered terrace and water pool have just as much bearing on the door through which they are seen as the interior house-treatment has in its relation to the same door. To take this door — for the sake of example — as a vantage point, is to show it as absolutely part of both the architectural- and the planting-detail. You cannot divorce it from either. Or suppose you have a fountain so symmetrically placed in the garden that it is seen through the open door from the interior of a library. Is it not as much a feature of the library embellishment as it is of the garden?

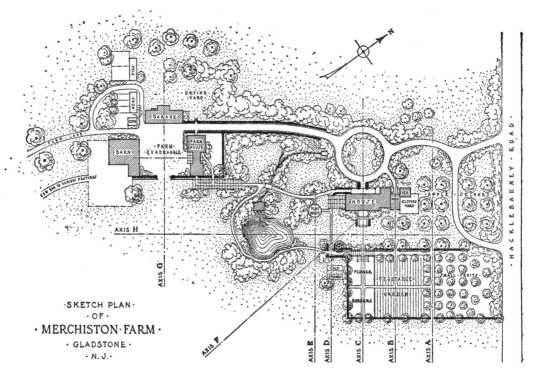

·SKETCH PLAN·
·OF·
· MERCHISTON·FARM ·
· GLADSTONE ·
· N. J.·

These facts, when realized, seem simple enough, but it is amazing to find how seldom they are planned from the start. It is this knowledge of the value of axis that is as essential to good landscape-gardening as it is to good architecture. The Italians of the Renaissance were past masters of this principle, as numberless villas testify. Instead of outdoor arrangement being uninvolved when related to the home, no matter how simple it may be, it should be involved and interrelated in just as many points and with as many logical sequences as can possibly be thought of without becoming confused. If it is confused, it is badly proportioned or planned.

The art involved in garden design requires technical knowledge as well as vision. We shall not have the beautiful and masterly gardening of Italy, France, and England in this country until we become more keen in our perception of the underlying anatomy of the plans upon which our fine plantings and placing of buildings are based. Never was the saying that "fools rush in where angels fear to tread" more applicable than in the vandalism of self-confident yet ignorant owners, who make meaningless and ill-advised arrangements in placing of buildings and in their plantings. The same effort and expense, whether simple or elaborate, would go further if a clearer conception of construction were more common, and a realization that — apart from the knowledge of the beauty of individual shrubs and trees — there is much to be learned in the underlying principles of the art of using them well. The greatest law involved as a starting point is that of the line of axis and a more picturesque treatment of it in relation to the problem as a whole.

BOBOLI GARDENS, FLORENCE

A MAJOR AXIS

VILLA CAMPANELI, TAORMINA

ONE OF FOUR RADIATING AXES FROM A CENTRE ENCLOSURE OF ARCHES
AND SEATS. AN INTIMATE AND INTERESTING GARDEN IN THE MIDST OF A
GROVE OF OVERGROWN TANGERINES

WHITEGATES FARM

A BROAD MARGIN OF TURF, INCLUDING TWO ROWS OF APPLE TREES, LIES
ABOUT THIS GARDEN ON THREE SIDES, THE HOUSE BEING ON THE FOURTH
SIDE. THIS FORMS AN ENCLOSURE BORDERED ON ONE SIDE BY THE LOW
GARDEN-HEDGE AND ON THE OTHER BY A LOW STONE WALL, PIERCED
BY GRILLE GATES OPPOSITE THE GARDEN PATHS. THE APPLE BOUGHS APPEAR–
ING BETWEEN THE EYE AND THE GARDEN PROPER, SEEN FROM THIS OUT-
LYING GREENSWARD, MAKE VERY INTERESTING AND VALUABLE NOTES IN
FOREGROUND COMPOSITION, NOT ONLY AT THE PERIODS OF BLOOM AND OF
FRUIT, BUT IN THE VERY FORM OF THE GNARLED BOUGHS THEMSELVES

SOSIEGO

ON THE MAJOR AXIS OF THE GARDEN ENCLOSURE

WHITEGATES FARM

ANOTHER EXAMPLE OF THE FOREGROUND GAINED BY APPLE TREES

WHITEGATES FARM

THE GARDEN, AS WELL AS THE HOME, WAS PLANNED ON THE EXACT AXIS OF
AN APPLE ORCHARD. THE VISTAS FROM PATHWAY OPENINGS BEING IN CON-
FORMITY WITH THE SPACES BETWEEN THE APPLE TREES, COMPOSITIONS IN
DISTANCE ARE POSSIBLE THROUGH EACH GRILLED GATEWAY

VILLA ALDOBRANDINI

NEARER DETAIL OF PAGE 61

VILLA ALDOBRANDINI

ILLUSTRATING AN IMPORTANT AXIS RUNNING FROM THE BANQUET-HALL
ACROSS THE FORECOURT TO A WALL FOUNTAIN WITH WATER CASCADES ABOVE.
SEE PAGE 62

VILLA ALDOBRANDINI

THE RUNWAY FOR WATER FROM THE RESERVOIR ABOVE TO THE SUCCESSION OF
CASCADES SEEN ON PAGE 61

THE LINDENS

SHOWING AXIS BETWEEN STREET GATE AND HOUSE DOOR

THE LINDENS

A NEARER DETAIL OF AXIS SHOWN ON PAGE 63

THE LINDENS

THE LONG AXIS, STARTING WITH THE GATEWAY (SEE PAGES 63 AND 64) AND
EXTENDING THROUGH A SEMISHADED GARDEN WITH OLD EVERGREENS
ABOUT IT, AND THROUGH A LONG FLOWER-GARDEN PATH BEYOND

THE LINDENS

FROM THE LONG FLOWER–PATH, LOOKING BACK TOWARD THE HOUSE, THROUGH THE SEMISHADED GARDEN SURROUNDED BY EVERGREENS. SEE PAGE 65

THE LINDENS

A NEARER VIEW, FROM THE DIAL TO THE DOOR AT THE BACK OF THE HALL

VILLA CAVALIERI
SEAT OF THE KNIGHTS
OF MALTA

AN INTERESTING ILLUSTRATION SHOWING THE IM-
PORTANCE OF AXIS MADE BY PLEACHED ALLEYS,
WHOSE OPENINGS CENTRE ON THE DOME OF ST.
PETER'S, FAR AWAY ACROSS THE CITY OF ROME.
(THIS IS DISCERNIBLE IN THE FIRST ILLUSTRATION;
IN THE OTHER, THE CAMERA FAILED TO INCLUDE IT.)
THE AXIS IS EFFECTIVE IN MAKING A BALANCED
AND COMPLETE COMPOSITION, SEEN THROUGH THE
KEYHOLE OF A GATE WHICH OPENS UPON THIS SHADY
PATHWAY

THE TAJ MAHAL, INDIA

UNDERCLIFF

THE SAME AXIS AS THAT SHOWN IN THE PLANTED GARDEN, BELOW. THE
GRADE IN EXCAVATION WAS LOWERED EIGHTEEN FEET AT THE END OF THE
GARDEN, THROUGH THE FORMATION OF THE "STERN AND ROCK–BOUND COAST"
OF THE NORTH SHORE. THE ARBOR, AS SEEN BELOW, WAS USED AS A LOGICAL
TERMINATION AND DISGUISE OF THE NECESSARILY AUSTERE RETAINING-WALL

UNDERCLIFF

AXIS OF THE GARDEN SEEN THROUGH ENTIRE LENGTH OF THE HOUSE, AND
CENTRING ON THE BREAKFAST-ROOM TABLE (SEE AXIS A, PAGE 11). THE
DROP IN LEVEL BETWEEN THE TERRACE AND THE GARDEN-TURF IS BUT
SIX INCHES AND COVERED BY ONE STEP, BUT THIS GIVES A DISTINCT IM-
PRESSION OF DEMARCATION BETWEEN THE GARDEN AND ITS SURROUNDINGS

UNDERCLIFF

THE FORECOURT, PLANTED MAINLY WITH RHODODENDRONS AND THORNS
THE HOUSE IS REACHED THROUGH THE NATURAL WOODED DRIVEWAY; ON THE
OTHER SIDE LIES THE SEA. SEE PAGE 11, AXIS E

UNDERCLIFF

THE CENTRAL DOORWAY OF THE HOUSE, ON WHICH THE GARDEN'S AXIS WAS
ESTABLISHED. TAKEN BEFORE PLANTING, FROM THE WOODED LAND AT THE
BACK OF THE GARDEN SITE. SEE PAGE 11, AXIS A

FERN HILL, BURLINGTON, VERMONT

THE LINE OF AXIS IN AN OLD GARDEN, CUTTING THROUGH THE DENSE SHADE OF SPRUCES BETWEEN THE FLOWER GARDEN AND THE VEGETABLE PLANTINGS BEYOND. THE SPACE IN SHADE UNDER THE TREES IS LARGE ENOUGH TO MOVE ABOUT WITH EASE. IT HOLDS TWO SEMICIRCULAR SEATS COMFORTABLY. THE FALLEN SPRUCE-NEEDLES ARE ALWAYS COOL UNDER ONE'S FEET AND THE BRILLIANCE OF THE FLOWERS SEEN FROM THIS SEMISHADE IS VERY RESTFUL AND CHARMING. FROM THE EXTREME END OF THE VEGETABLE GARDEN BEYOND, THE GLIMPSE OF COLOR SEEN THROUGH THE SPRUCES IS INTER-ESTING. THIS WAS MADE BY THE CAREFUL CUTTING OF BUT FOUR SPRUCE LIMBS, THE REST OF THE BRANCHES FORMING THE NATURAL ENCLOSURE

MERCHISTON FARM

THE TREATMENT OF AN INFORMAL APPROACH TO THE HOUSE

MERCHISTON FARM

THE SAME PATHWAY FROM THE OPPOSITE DIRECTION

73

A FLORENTINE VILLA

HIGHWALL

FROM GARDEN SEAT TO THE SEA. SEE PAGE 49, AXIS G

HIGHWALL
SEE PAGE 49; AXIS E

A GREEN-TERRACE TREATMENT IN RELATION TO AN IMPORTANT
DOOR OF THE HOUSE

COURTESY OF WILLIAM S. RICHARDSON, ESQ., CHESTER, NEW JERSEY

MAUDESLEIGH
ONE OF THE MINOR AXES OF THE GARDEN

The Use of
THE HEDGE

III

THE USE OF THE HEDGE

EDGES might be described as that formality of green growth most nearly related to architecture. Indeed, there is so very fine a line between their artificially produced form and proportion and that of an architectural detail that practically they may be thought of as part of the general architectural scheme. It is the meeting-point of architecture and the green world — one of the instances where Nature, harnessed to civilization, does not lose in value. We might compare the hedge to the magic — though artificial — touch which transforms the great forest tree, with all its freedom of growth and beauty of line, into a splendidly wrought column, so full of proportion and dignity that the sisters of the forest, from which it came, might almost envy it.

The hedge is essentially artificial in its original treatment and also in its preservation, and left untouched for a short period, goes back with amazing alacrity to the freer growth which the Lord intended.

Let us begin with our low flower-bed borders, our box and our barberry, and think of them as hedges. They are the little ones, and they creep up in size to those which we look over — which are of enormous use — and to those which are higher than ourselves ; and then we begin to think of the stately hedges of box and holly in Scotland and England, and the wonderful yew and ilex hedges which we find in Italy — the backgrounds for the statues ; the enclosures for the amphitheatres ; the protecting walls behind which romance and intrigue have been born and cardinals have walked.

81

THE SPIRIT OF THE GARDEN

The hedge is no upstart; it has accentuated scenes of splendor from the earliest times of planting. It has lent itself as gracefully to the merrymakings of the maze as to the gardens of the Roman Emperors.

The great note of all the famous villas of Italy — so wonderful in their outline and proportion that no flowers are needed to make them gardens — is the perfect harmony of idea between the architectural details of steps, pools, and pathways and the walls formed by hedges.

The use of the hedge is a very valuable asset which came into existence as civilization advanced to the point where man first grasped the idea of privacy and individuality about his home. In the very earliest records of gardens there are illustrations of the hedge in the quaintest perspective.

The hedge is an accent, first and foremost, and its purpose is either a background or a barrier. Being artificial, it of necessity should be planted in relation to architecture — that term being used to denote the formalities of garden or parterre arrangement as well as of the buildings proper. A hedge must have a purpose, just as much as a balustrade or a flight of steps; it must be in proportion to its environment, just as much as the house or its garden. It should be looked upon, where it is used as a background, purely as a flat surface against which the informal growth of flowers or the moving figures of people are accentuated. When considered in the larger scheme, where trees in the distance and the perspective of diminishing lines are seen in relation to it, its own sharp outline becomes an important factor. Therefore, two uses are found in the same hedge: in relation to smaller things it is a background, and in relation to larger things, an accent. When planted in front of old trees, the hedge makes in its contrast, in rigidity of form, a note so firm and controlled as to accentuate the freedom of growth in the trees. It lends a note of variety while suggesting an important one in composition.

THE USE OF THE HEDGE

As a barrier, the hedge is of practical use and more pleasing to the eye than any other form of fencing. Its most important use is found when planted in front of the houses on a village street. It gives to the street itself, as does nothing else, a style in composition; and from the owner's view within the grounds it makes the place seem larger and more important by cutting off the highway as well as providing a background.

When service-wings of houses lie in close proximity to the garden or terrace, and privacy must be secured though there is limited space, the hedge is of great advantage, as a strip of land from four to six feet wide is all that is needed to screen off that part of the house and to create a background for the terrace or the garden.

In the plantings of gardens, clipped blocks of hedge may be introduced for the purpose of accent or contrast at the crossing of paths and sides of gateways, or other blocks as backgrounds for seats or fountains. Niches for the placing of statues are frequently found abroad cut into the surface of the hedge and are sometimes carried out in this country with marked success. In the bounding of terraces, where used alone or planted behind a balustrade, a hedge is always dignified, and an important note.

There is a prevalent idea that hedges require great time and care in this country where very high wages are to be considered, but anyone who has had them knows that for what they lend in effect they take comparatively little time. If a hedge is well kept from the beginning, three to six clippings a year are all that are required for the most vigorous. We spend an infinitely greater proportion of time on vast extent of lawns, in relation to the amount of pleasure we derive from them. If there is to be any choice in the things which require labor, do without some unnecessary areas of lawn which take weekly attention, and give a fraction of that labor to hedges.

83

Climbing roses, if not allowed too much liberty in their growth, make a wonderfully lovely hedge when grown over some artificial support of the shape and height required. Hornbeam, cherry, dogwood, laburnum, arborvitæ, and dozens of other small trees lend themselves easily to being bent into the form of hedge-like arbors, and with so delightful an effect, that one wonders the charming sense of frolic and surprise is not more sought after by us all. Why are we so contented to pass from one scheme of arrangement to another through barren treatment, when it takes but a hedged-in walk to give us the sensation of a marked place-apart, and makes all the difference in the world in the overlapping interests to be gained by a bit of imagination?

Is there nothing more to be desired in the formal approach to a garden than a gravel path, flanked with the neatly kept turf-edging of a lawn? The path, it is true, is the only bare necessity; but is that all we have to consider? Suppose the path is looked upon as but the backbone of the approach, and we add a broad hedge of great height on either hand, perhaps so planted that three to six feet of margin are left on each side of the pathway for shade-loving flowers? We thus create shadows, a mossy path, an invitation for birds, an increased sense of distance, a vanishing point in perspective, an added lovable feature about our home; and the pathway has been made a romantic introduction of shade between two interesting open spaces. Children grown to men and women fifty years after will remember the spot with a glow of mystery and pleasure, whereas the barren, well-kept path would be quite forgotten. If a pathway for some reason should not be bordered by a high unbroken line of this kind, it can be flanked by regularly or irregularly planted shrubs, placed as far apart as desired. Cedars, dwarf fruits, thorns, or poplars all form beautiful path-margins of a broken formal type. In England I remember a wonderful hedge on either side of a wide grass-path joining an artist's studio, which was built on the edge of a little wooded piece of land, and his garden, which was by his house some distance away. The path lay in a graceful curve through a grain-field terminating at the studio door. The hedge was formed of sweetbriar rose, kept clipped to a rounded top, standing about four to five feet high. The perfume from the young shoots was pungent and delightful as one passed along the path, and the ripening grain, seen on either side of it, made a fine waving background for the bright green color and formal outline of the hedge.

Clipped perpendicular walls of hedge can be made when a pathway should be introduced through tall swamp- or wild wooded-growth. By introducing a dense natural planting of high-bush blueberry, clethra, the various viburnums and thorns, wild roses, azaleas, barberry, and spice-bush, and by constantly cutting their growth to a true vertical line on each side of the path, a tall and interesting enclosure for a green walk can be formed in a few years. The constant pruning induces a vigor of growth on the face of the green wall which is very beautiful. A consistent choice of natural plants can in this way create a feature leading from one important point to another. The setting of a house, for instance, can — with no false introduction of planting — be connected with an equally architectural garden or tennis court, through a stretch of natural woodland which demands some continuity of treatment.

When entrances through hedges are to be cut in semicircular or "vaulted" arches, it is well to have a frame made of the desired shape and have the hedge-opening cut by this frame year after year. Curved lines when left to the accuracy of the eye are not true, and the general outline suffers in consequence. Our old, much abused friend, the privet, is so inexpensive and so dependable that no one is left with an excuse for going

85

without a hedge wherever one can be tucked in. Arborvitæ, buckthorn, hemlock, hornbeam, barberry, beech, and some of the viburnums are more to be desired when one's choice alone is to be considered. Nothing is more tranquil than the quality of green form which good hedge-pruning gives to a composition, and it is far better to have a thousand feet of privet than a few hundred feet of some rarer hedge. The composition comes first and the material used, second, in the importance of hedges.

BOBOLI GARDENS, FLORENCE
GREEN WALLS FORMED BY CLIPPED SHRUBBERY

OLDFIELDS

HEDGE OF HEMLOCK AS A BACKGROUND WITH BOX EDGING USED ON GRASS
PATHS. NOTE THE LACK OF ALL HARD TURF-TRIMMING BETWEEN IT AND
BOX BORDER

MERCHISTON FARM

INFORMAL HEDGE TREATMENT BETWEEN HOUSE DRIVE AND FARM BUILDINGS.
SEE PLAN. PAGE 52

HIGHWALL

FOUR ILLUSTRATIONS SHOWING USE OF HEDGES AND WALLS TO FORM OUTER
BOUNDARY, INNER COURT, FORECOURT, AND SCREEN PLANTINGS
NO. 1. ENTRANCE TO FORECOURT. SEE PAGE 49, AXIS A

HIGHWALL

HEDGE TREATMENT ON EACH SIDE OF ENTRANCE DRIVE. HEDGE OF VIBURNUM
DENTATUM. SEE PAGE 49, AXIS A

HIGHWALL

OPPOSITE SIDE OF DRIVE, AT TIME OF PLANTING STABLE AND GARAGE—THE
ENTRANCE TO THE LATTER BEING ON THE STREET SIDE. SEE PAGE 49

HIGHWALL

AXIS FROM HOUSE DOOR THROUGH WALL TO FACE OF GARAGE, WHICH WAS USED
AS A BACKGROUND. SEE ILLUSTRATION ABOVE, ALSO PAGE 49, AXIS B

HADRIAN'S VILLA, TIVOLI

HADRIAN'S VILLA, TIVOLI

HADRIAN'S VILLA, TIVOLI

CROWHURST

CROWHURST

TWO ILLUSTRATIONS OF A FORMAL PLANTING OF ARBORVITÆ USED IN THE
GARDEN AND AGAIN INTRODUCED IN THE INTERIOR OF THE HALL, BRINGING
THE FEELING OF THE GARDEN DIRECTLY INTO THE HOUSE

MAUDESLEIGH

TREATMENT OF DRIVEWAY APPROACHING HOUSE FLANKED BY ARBORVITÆ.
THE WIDE MARGIN ON EITHER SIDE—TURF TERMINATING IN A HEDGE LINE—
GIVES A COMPOSITION TO THE DRIVEWAY ITSELF AND AT THE SAME TIME ACCEN-
TUATES THE FREER GROWTH OF THE TREES BEHIND IT

MAUDESLEIGH

FIVE ILLUSTRATIONS SHOWING ORIGINAL HILL ON WHICH, FOR VARIOUS REASONS,
IT WAS BEST TO PLACE THE NEW GARDENS, WATER TOWER, AND GREENHOUSES
EXISTING. THE HILL-PLANTING ABOUT THE GARDEN ENCLOSURE WAS MADE OF
NATIVE TREES AND PLANTS AS DESCRIBED ON PAGE 173. THEIR GROWTH HAS
EVENTUALLY OBLITERATED THE WATER TOWER FROM VIEW AND LENT THE
OPPORTUNITY FOR A CLIPPED PERPENDICULAR WALL
I. GARDEN WALLS BEGUN

MAUDESLEIGH

II. SITE AFTER FIVE YEARS

MAUDESLEIGH

III. APPROACH TOWARD GARDEN ON AXIS TO GARDEN ENTRANCE, BEFORE
PLANTING

MAUDESLEIGH

IV. TOWARD GARDEN ENTRANCE. ILLUSTRATES WALLED WALK OF NATURAL
CLIPPED GROWTH FORMING THE CONNECTING FEATURE BETWEEN HOUSE AND
GARDENS. SEE ILLUSTRATION V FOR SAME GATEWAY

MAUDESLEIGH

V. GATES AT EACH END OF THE CENTRAL PART OF THE UPPER GARDENS. GREEN-
HOUSES BEYOND THE CLIPPED HEDGE

MAUDESLEIGH

EIGHT ILLUSTRATIONS SHOWING USE OF SALIX PENTANDRA HEDGE, PLANTED
TO CUT OFF EXISTING GREENHOUSES FROM SITE OF GARDENS. OVAL CLIPPINGS
IN GATEWAYS EMPLOYED AND A GREENHOUSE YARD CREATED. SEE PAGE 173.
AFTER PASSING THROUGH THE ENTRANCE GRILLE–GATE (PAGE 98), THE LONG
GARDEN–PATH TO THE OPPOSITE SIMILAR GATEWAY WAS OF NECESSITY CON-
FRONTED BY THE GREENHOUSES, AT THE TIME THE GARDENS AND APPROACH
WERE MADE

I. DURING WORK
II. FIRST PLANTING

MAUDESLEIGH

III. SALIX HEDGE BEFORE IT REACHED FULL GROWTH

MAUDESLEIGH

IV. HEDGE CLIPPED. TAKEN FROM SIDE PATH OF UPPER GARDEN. ILLUSTRATING
THE COMPLETE SCREENING OF GREENHOUSES WHERE BUT EIGHTEEN INCHES OF
PLANTING SPACE WERE GIVEN. SEE PAGES 83 AND 173

MAUDESLEIGH

V. GREENHOUSE YARD BEFORE HEDGE REACHED FULL HEIGHT
SEE PAGE 173

MAUDESLEIGH

VI. TO UPPER GARDEN FROM GREENHOUSE-YARD ENTRANCE
OPPOSITE NO. III, PAGE 100

MAUDESLEIGH
VII. ROSE GARDEN AT TIME OF PLANTING

MAUDESLEIGH
VIII. SAME AS NO. VII, WHEN MATURE

CRAIGIE HOUSE

TWO ILLUSTRATIONS, BEFORE AND AFTER PLANTING, SHOWING THE USE OF
THE TRELLIS FOR VERY RAPID EFFECT IN CUTTING OUT SOME OBJECTIONABLE
FEATURE OR MAKING A GARDEN DEMARCATION WHERE NO SPACE COULD BE
GIVEN TO THE GROWTH OF A HEDGE. THE OLD STABLE, USUALLY THE HAUNT
OF NUMBERLESS PIGEONS, LENT INTEREST TO THE GARDEN WHEN SEEN IN
PART ONLY. THE LATTICE USED IN THIS WAY SHOULD BE ENTIRELY COVERED
BY GREEN, KEPT WELL-CLIPPED IN FORM. THE OPENING IN THE HEDGE-FENCE
(SEE PAGE 105) WAS MADE OF THE ORIGINAL DOORFRAME TAKEN FROM THE
HOUSE IN PORTLAND, MAINE, WHERE LONGFELLOW WAS BORN. THE DESIGN
IN BOX EDGING WAS RESET IN ITS PERSIAN PATTERN EXACTLY AS THE POET
HAD ORIGINALLY DESIGNED IT WHEN THE GARDEN WAS ADDED TO CRAIGIE
HOUSE BY HIM

CRAIGIE HOUSE

II. AFTER PLANTING

A PLEACHED ALLEY

Photograph from M. E. Hewitt Studio, New York

WELWYN

THE IMPORTANCE OF THE GREEN ENCLOSURE OF A GARDEN

PEACOCKS AT WARWICK CASTLE, ENGLAND

A REAR VIEW AND FRONT VIEW. THE BIRDS SEEMED TO KNOW HOW IMPOR-
TANT THEY LOOKED AGAINST THE FINELY KEPT HEDGE, AS THEY LITERALLY
"STOOD FOR THEIR PHOTOGRAPHS" THE MOMENT THEY SAW THE CAMERA

VILLA D'ESTE

PLANTING FORMING GREEN CLIPPED WALL

FONTAINEBLEAU

HEDGE LINE IN TREE FORMATION

VILLA PALMIERI, ITALY

SHOWING THE VALUE OF BACKGROUND IN A HEDGE

110

VILLA MEDICI, ROME

Photograph from M. E. Hewitt Studio, New York

WELWYN
THE USE OF PLENTY OF GREEN, ACCENTED WITH FLOWERS

ARBORS and GATEWAYS

IV

ARBORS AND GATEWAYS

HE arbor may be classed as of the same type of importance as the hedge — another link between architecture and the green world — and be looked upon, when used in connection with a hedge, as its gateway or doorway. This may be of a depth like that of the hedge or it may be repeated again and again to border the line of a long pathway, thus forming the pleached alley, which we rarely see in this country but frequently see abroad. It is the single arbor repeated at close plantings across a broad pathway, forming a long covered green walk of symmetry, and proportion, and often dense shade. This may easily become the most intimate and enchanting spot about a home, by bringing two otherwise unrelated features together, while it only requires the space of the pathway.

There are enormous numbers of shrubs, vines, and trees which adapt themselves well to the purposes of the arbor and there are no end of ways that our small fruits can — by different treatment than is ordinarily used in their planting — be made to contribute formal, decorative features about the house and garden, and become a source of pleasure instead of ranking as merely utilitarian. To take grapes for example, as a vine: how often these are grown on rows of wire in the vegetable garden, when, if grown on an arbor adjoining the house, terrace, or gardens, the spot becomes a definite feature in the effect and the pleasure derived from it. There is nothing lovelier than the young forming green fruit and leaves of grapes, with the sun shining through them, making patches of light and shadow on the pathway of brick or stone pavement below. The vines can be perfectly cared for from the practical aspect — in pruning, spraying, and picking — and the grapevines serve two purposes.

Let us take the dwarf fruits, for another example, like apples, pears, cherries, and so forth, which can be made into delightful arbors. When grown in conformity with the necessary supports, they may be planted on each side of a pathway leading from a garden to a child's playhouse; from a terrace to a tennis court; or from any one of a thousand starting-points to some other spot which should be carefully connected, and thereby create a feature which is a real pleasure. The fruit is easily picked, and at the time of bloom the long arbor makes a world of beauty at the moment in spring when we are most alive to it.

I once saw a very wonderful arbor of laburnum in England, running a great length on either side of a garden. The effect in perspective was charming, as the arbor was very wide. The trusses of yellow bloom hung down in a glory of color. The use of the laburnum would be possible here if not attempted too far north, but the same effect can be easily gained by white or purple wistaria. Flowering dogwood and hornbeam bend easily to conform to any inconspicuous frame which establishes the shape of an arbor, and in their growth completely hide the frame. An informal arbor is successful made of upright posts of natural wood (without the bark), and the overhanging beams made of rough old fence-rails, their uneven surface and gray color creating a remarkable background and complement for all the vines and their bloom. An arbor was made in this way on a little hillside adjoining our own very informal garden and some farm buildings. The pathway, dropping off constantly in grade, was relieved in its monotony by flat field-stones used at intervals as steps, and the arbor itself was constructed in marked levels as it ascended the grade. The first stage of bareness was overcome by the use of annual gourds, which made so successful a covering the first year, that we watched the permanent growth develop almost with regret. Turkeys, perching there in the moonlight, looked like peacocks among the long green and yellow gourds which hung in profusion in their exquisitely formed annual growth. The other vines which ultimately covered the arbor were, however, planted, and by the next year war would have raged if the permanent growth had been encroached upon by the upstart annual — however beautiful the gourds may have proved themselves. The vines used as a cover are Dr. Van Fleet and Silver Moon rose, white wistaria, a touch of *Akebia*, and *Vitis heterophylla* with its turquoise-blue berry to give color in the early autumn. A few old woody vines of large blue grapes were moved to the arbor to lend a gnarled effect, though soon enough the great thorny runners of the Silver Moon rose gave ample growth of that nature. In one spot the *Forsythia suspensa* was so near — in the embankment-planting through which the arbor passes — that it has been allowed to climb up into the arbor and has proved a most delightful note of color in the early spring before the wistaria blooms, its long limp growth falling down from the rafters. It sounds like a riot. It is, though, a pleasant one. The sides of the pathway under the arbor are bordered by German iris. Little gray bird-houses are fastened to the gray upright posts and suet is nailed to them all winter. The outcome is that now not only is there bloom throughout the season, but this gentle ascent in the semishade is restful and inviting, and the spot is filled with birds. The flowers in the garden below, seen from its shade, are interesting in contrast. One of the farm buildings, with casement windows and doorway opening into the arbor, lies at the far end, thus giving another proof of the possibility of joining together two otherwise

117

unrelated features. The transition between the personal part of our home and the farm part was in this way blended into a graceful change of environment without a jarring note; a rather difficult drop in grade was overcome; and an excuse was made for the use of an arbor which otherwise might easily never have existed.

Plants which lend themselves to arbors of this kind are *Tecoma grandiflora*, that gorgeous trumpet-flower so superior to the common variety; various climbing roses; grapes, edible and non-edible; bittersweet; carefully chosen varieties of clematis and *Wistaria Chinensis* with not only its exquisite and fragrant bloom but its light-green velvety seed-pods, which are equally decorative. If any garden-planter does not know of the non-edible grape, the *Vitis heterophylla*—sometimes listed as Ampelopsis—with its small berries which are produced simultaneously in a range of colors in the same little bunch, let this inadequate description recommend its use. (This comes in a variegated leaf, which is ugly in comparison to the green-leaf variety and should be avoided.) The berries appearing late in the season are in clusters of turquoise-blue, purple, slate-gray, green, and speckled white. The leaf is exceedingly interesting in its deeply lobed outline. Though the growth is rampant, once it is established, it can be kept in control by the same method of very vigorous pruning as that applied to ordinary grape-culture. A heavy cutting-back to within two buds of the old wood is necessary, and during the summer, if the long tendrils become too aggressive they can be pinched off at will.

Great care should always be used to prevent the top growth of an arbor from ever becoming completely covered and matted in its overlapping growth. The interlacing branches with glimpses of sky and light between are too important to be lost; a thick mass of green leafage deprives one of that translucent quality of color gained by light through the green leaves. On the other hand, the form and construction of the arbor itself, either in its uprights or its overhead beams, should never be lost by too unbroken a mass of foliage. Judicious pruning — even the annihilation of much good growth — is often very important, when it hides the columns or beams of an arbor too completely.

The use of the "rustic" cedar arbors and seats should be forever tabooed! Their incongruous ugliness is bad enough, and with its incidental slaughter of one of the most decorative and lovely of trees, which in living form can play so great a part in our gardens and their environment, should be looked upon by garden-makers with a frown. The rustic arbor belongs to the mid-Victorian age, marked by fashions — practically dead to-day — of geranium flower-beds, red salvia and canna plantings, and palms in jardinières. The vandal who still deals in the trunks of cedars for arbor-making and garden furniture marks a last remnant of that period which we may call the Slough of Despond. He will eventually die out only through the lack of demand for his pilfered material.

Various forms of upright columns in plaster, brick, wood, and stone lend themselves well to the support of plants and as a background for vines which should grow around them. Visible wires — which in some cases act as additional support — are incongruous, unless they are merely used to ensure proper aid until such time as the vine is old enough to have caught its growth well into the overhead beams and so have secured its own permanency. The uprights should never be too matted with vine for the best arbor-effect, for the outline of gnarled woody growth appearing against a column of gray stucco or mossy brick is finer than against a background of layers of its own growth. A column which is worth building is worth seeing, though on the other hand, it should never look crude and naked by the vine growth being allowed to grow entirely on the top of the arbor.

As with all entrances, the approach to an arbor may, by plantings, be led up to gradually if the best effect is to be made. To enter a long arbor abruptly reminds one of a train, as from the open it suddenly dashes into a tunnel; and to emerge in the same way — abruptly, with no setting about it — is a mistake. We see this too often, and it gives the arbor the appearance of being unrelated to its surroundings, and robbed of all rhythm in its arrangement. A flanking of green growth in shrub-massing, formal cedars, or the horizontal branches of a spreading low tree, may break the austere beginning or end of an arbor.

The pleached alley planted of privet makes a quick and very dense arbor-walk and, as at Sosiego, carried on each side of the long garden, makes a background for the flowers which looks like a hedge, pierced at the various axes of pathways by side openings. People appear and disappear from or into its shady vaulted enclosure, and the length of its planting is great enough to make its vanishing points at the ends brilliant spots of light and color. Moss collects on the trunks of the shrubs, and the path under its shade is of a bronze green and always damp. Though this arbor is of the commonest of plants, this one — of privet — has given no end of pleasure and has added a very important note to a garden which — in the truest sense of the use of a garden — was lived in daily for many years.

ITALY
THE PLEACHED ALLEY OF LIVE OAK AT CASTELLO AND PETRAJA

UNDERCLIFF

DETAIL OF ARBOR TREATMENT WHEN FULLY DEVELOPED. SEE PLAN, PAGE 11;
ALSO PAGE 70

UNDERCLIFF

PATHWAY LEADING TO GRAPE ARBOR, WHICH SPANS THE GARDEN AT ITS END.
SEE PLAN, PAGE 11; ALSO PAGE 70. BIRD BATH BY FRANCES GRIMES, SCULPTOR

UNDERCLIFF

THE WALLED TERMINATION OF THE TERRACE, TREATED WITH ESPALIER FRUIT
AND A CLOSED–DOOR GATEWAY

PALERMO, SICILY
PLEACHED DRIVEWAY

ROME
AN INTERESTING OVERHEAD–ARCH TREATMENT OF CLIPPED LIVE–OAK TREES,
FRAMING ST. PETER'S IN THE DISTANCE

VILLA PALMIERI

GATE DETAIL

AN ORNAMENTAL ITALIAN GRAPE–ARBOR

FRASCATI

TWO ITALIAN GATES—ONE SEEN THROUGH THE OTHER—WITH A ROAD BETWEEN

FRASCATI

AN ITALIAN GATEWAY

MAUDESLEIGH

DETAIL IN THE ROSE GARDEN

MAUDESLEIGH

HALF OF THE SEMICIRCULAR ROSE-ARBOR AS THE TERMINATION OF THE ROSE
GARDEN

MAUDESLEIGH

IN THE UPPER FLOWER–GARDEN. DETAIL OF THE PERGOLA CONSTRUCTION
BEFORE IT BECAME MORE DENSELY COVERED BY THE VINE (Actinidia arguta)

MAUDESLEIGH

A DETAIL OF WOODEN GARDEN–GATES, AFTERWARD REPLACED BY GRILLE
GATES

MAUDESLEIGH

DETAIL IN THE UPPER GARDEN

MAUDESLEIGH

UNDER THE PERGOLA IN THE UPPER GARDEN

SOSIEGO

THE ARBOR OF NATURAL UNCUT LOCUST-WOOD CONSTRUCTION COVERED BY
GRAPEVINES AND ROSES

MAUDESLEIGH

ONE OF THE GATEWAYS IN THE UPPER GARDEN

WHITEGATES FARM

THE INTERSECTION OF TWO PATHWAYS JOINED BY AN ARBOR. THE UPRIGHTS
OF PIPING (EVENTUALLY OBLITERATED) ARE USED ONLY AS A FRAME FOR THE
VINES WHICH INTERLACE OVERHEAD

SOSIEGO

FROM AN OPENING IN THE PLEACHED ALLEY. SEE PAGE 120

SOSIEGO

THE GRAPE- AND ROSE-ARBOR

CROWHURST

ARCHES OF ARBORVITÆ ON BOTH SIDES OF THE POOL.   SEE PAGE 84

CROWHURST

DETAIL SHOWING THE ARBORVITÆ ARCHES IN CONSTRUCTION AND EARLY
GROWTH. SMALL BENT PIPES WERE USED AS A SUPPORT IN ESTABLISHING THE
FORM OF THE TREES, WHICH LATER WERE SEVERELY CLIPPED

CROWHURST

GATEWAY WHERE THE GARDEN JOINS THE NATURAL WOODED GROWTH OF
GNARLED PINES AND NATIVE SHRUBS

CROWHURST

A GARDEN GATE

CROWHURST

GATEWAY LEADING INTO FARM COURT

AN ITALIAN GATEWAY

MERCHISTON FARM
DETAIL OF ANNUAL GOURDS

MERCHISTON FARM

LOOKING DOWN THE ARBOR, SHOWING THE OVERHEAD BEAMS OF NATURAL OLD
POST–RAILS

MERCHISTON FARM

THE SITE WHICH LENT ITSELF TO THE ARBOR, ILLUSTRATING THE ADVANTAGE
TAKEN OF A NATURALLY UGLY CHANGE IN LEVELS.   PHOTOGRAPH TAKEN FROM
POINT ON INTERSECTION OF AXIS D AND AXIS H.   SEE PAGE 52

MERCHISTON FARM

USE OF AN ARCH IN BRINGING ICE-HOUSE AND DRYING-GROUND INTO RELATION
WITH SERVICE END OF HOUSE.   SEE AXIS B, PAGE 52

MERCHISTON FARM
PATH INTO ARBOR AT SOUTH OF HOUSE ON AXIS D. SEE PLAN, PAGE 52

MERCHISTON FARM
IN THE INFORMAL GARDEN

MERCHISTON FARM

FROM THE FLOWER–PLANTING BELOW TOWARD THE ASCENDING ARBOR

MERCHISTON FARM

IN THE ARBOR IN ROSE TIME

MERCHISTON FARM

AFTER THE WHITE WISTARIA HAD BECOME ESTABLISHED

MERCHISTON FARM

THE ARBOR IN ITS FIRST YEAR, COVERED WITH GOURDS, TAKEN FROM ITS UPPER
END WHERE IT "TIES" THE GARDEN BELOW INTO THE FARM BUILDINGS

147

FRASCATI

THE GATEWAY OF ALDOBRANDINI

TO TERMINATE A PATHWAY BY A WELL–PLANNED ARCH MAKES FOR A VALUABLE
NOTE IN COMPOSITION.   THE ARCH, HOWEVER, MUST ALWAYS BE INTRODUCED
IN A WALL OR A HEDGE–LINE. A GATEWAY OR ARBOR IS AN OPENING, AND SHOULD
BE RELATED TO ITS SETTING

EXAMPLE OF POOR ARBOR–CONCEPTION

THE VINES SHOULD FORM THE TOP SHADE, THEIR SUPPORT BEING THE CROSS
BEAMS, WHOSE ONLY REASON FOR EXISTING IS FOR THIS PURPOSE. TO CREATE
A FALSE SHADE BY MEDIOCRE CARPENTRY AND THEN COVER IT, IS LIKE TRIM-
MING A PARASOL, ALL TRUE RELATION BETWEEN THE USE OF THE ROSES AND
THEIR SUPPORT IN THE FORMATION OF THE ARBOR BEING MISSED

A GRAPE ARBOR OF AMPLE WIDTH WHICH SPREADS OVER LILY–
AND IRIS–PLANTINGS ON EITHER SIDE OF THE PATHWAY

WELWYN

DESCENDING INTO THE ARBOR

AN ARBOR OF LABURNUM IN ENGLAND
SEE PAGE 116

CRAIGIE HOUSE

COLONIAL MOTIVE IN ARBOR AND GATES, WITH LOCUST TREES, LARKSPUR, AND
HUMMING BIRDS

CRAIGIE HOUSE

THE ARBOR FROM THE GARDEN. SEE PAGES 156, 157

CRAIGIE HOUSE

LOOKING BACK FROM REAR OF PROPERTY THROUGH ARBOR TOWARD GARDEN
GATE

CRAIGIE HOUSE

FROM UNDER THE ARBOR, OUT INTO THE GARDEN AND LOOKING TOWARD THE
HOUSE

CRAIGIE HOUSE

GARDEN ARBOR THROUGH GATEWAY. THIS ARBOR SERVES THREE PURPOSES:
(1) IT FORMS A SHADY SPOT WHICH IS LARGE ENOUGH FOR A GROUP OF PEOPLE TO
SIT IN; (2) IT MAKES THE LONG PATH MORE PICTURESQUE, BREAKING THE EFFECT
OF UNINTERESTING DISTANCE; (3) IT CREATES A CAMOUFLAGE SCREENING A
NEIGHBOR'S BUILDING WHICH LIES AT THE DIRECT REAR OF THE ARBOR. SEE
PAGE 155 FOR THEIR RELATION IN EFFECT

FROM THE GARDEN TOWARD THE BACK OF CRAIGIE HOUSE

CRAIGIE HOUSE

GATEWAYS TO THE GARDEN, THE COLONIAL MOTIVE BEING USED TO CONFORM
TO THE OLD HOUSE. SEE PAGE 157

HIGHWALL

FROM THE PICKING–GARDEN OF FLOWERS THROUGH AN ARCHED LILAC HEDGE
TO THE FIRST FORECOURT GATE. ACROSS THE FORECOURT IS SEEN ANOTHER
GATE OPENING ON A TURF PATH EDGED BY HORNBEAM, WHICH WAS PLANTED TO
FORM A PLEACHED ALLEY
NOTE THE ADVANTAGE OF ONE SCHEME BEING FOLLOWED BY ANOTHER IN PRO-
DUCING A SENSE OF DISTANCE IN A VERY SMALL AREA. SEE AXIS D, PAGE 49

HIGHWALL

A SECOND ILLUSTRATION, THE REVERSE OF ABOVE, SHOWING THE ADVANTAGE
GAINED IN A MASS OF BLOOM IN THE PICKING–GARDEN, SEEN THROUGH TWO
GATES, THE LILAC–HEDGE ARCH AND ACROSS THE FORECOURT

IN THE OLD GARDEN OF FERN HILL, BURLINGTON, VERMONT

OLDFIELDS

A SLIGHT RISE OF TWO STEPS AND AN ARCH MAKE A DISTINCT DEMARCA-
TION FOR THE LITTLE GARDEN BEYOND, WHICH IS ON A SMALLER SCALE

VILLA PALMIERI, FLORENCE

AN ARBOR OF FRUIT TREES

OLDFIELDS

AN ARBOR,—NOT COMPLETELY COVERED AT THE TIME THE PHOTOGRAPH WAS
TAKEN,—SHOWING ITS IMPORTANCE IN THE TERMINATION OF THE GARDEN
WHILE, IN REALITY, THE LINE OF PATHWAY IS LEFT QUITE OPEN

PALERMO, SICILY
IN AN OLD CLOISTER

GREENHOUSES

V

GREENHOUSES

RIVATE greenhouses, while the acme of all things desirable to the gardener in charge, are — we will hope, in the minds of those who are guided by beauty — the most artificial and hopelessly ugly utilitarian blot that has perforce to be placed on an estate. While we may appreciate to the full the individual plant, beautifully grown and available at a period when flowering plants can only be grown artificially, we never really enjoy them until they are brought out of their forcing surroundings into the more personal setting of our homes; and yet this transference is in most cases disadvantageous to the bloom and to the general condition of the plant for future use. There are rare instances where the taste for the fresh green leaf and the blooming plant has been so blended with the true feeling for the fitness of environment that a greenhouse has been created to act as an enclosed space, where sunlight and summer air are, as it were, entrapped and held over through the bleak days of frost, and where the general sense of the conservatory — as we usually think of it — has been lost in the true beauty of a well-managed scheme and has filled and satisfied a genuine need through the winter months.

I remember an old Georgian house in Virginia where one of the two wings had been constructed as an orangery through which one passed to a room beyond. This enclosure was architecturally beautiful — the interior walls being formed of stone, as was the exterior of the house — and lighted entirely from floor to ceiling by its glass-enclosed sides. There was no top light, but the unusual height of ceiling gave one a sense of air and atmosphere. The blue of the sky with its clouds and its storms, seen through the orange leaves, was quite visible through the height of the side glass. A certain ugly glare which comes through all glass-topped buildings was thus avoided, and with the passing hours the light, coming from one side and then the other, cast changing shadows on the cool stone floor. One of the blank walls held a beautiful wall-fountain which gave only the least suspicion of sound as it filled its semicircular basin. The orange and lemon trees were old and had never been pruned to any compact monotony of growth. Their branches stretched aloft and horizontally and one passed through them in many places. An occasional mass of color was seen here and there, occuring spasmodically with the blooming of some plant. The predominating note was of green growth, luxuriant, succulent, seductively full of odor, and an unexpected blooming branch, spray, or single flower lent an illusive flitting sense of coquetry to the place. This introduction of bloom was at one season gained by unpruned single azalea plants—some free in growth and with high gnarled woody stems, others branching low and even spreading out on the stone floor in their undergrowth. Everything here was in tubs, as I remember, and yet so delightfully arranged that there was very little sense of stilted artificiality. Perhaps many of the tubs were sunken; they might easily have been, but I cannot recall this feature. It is needless to tell what the fragrance was in passing through this enclosure and even in the adjoining rooms, when incessant orange buds were forming and the pungent fruit, if touched in passing, lent added variety in spiciness.

Splendid opportunities are often lost for forming a transitional space between one room and another — as the approach to the dining-room or the living-room, or the library — by an enclosed loggia filled with green, where a change of atmosphere and of condition is so marked that it makes, as it were, a punctuation or an exclamation point in the architectural arrangement of a house that otherwise becomes monotonous in its lack of anything to break the housed-in feeling. Perhaps one reason why this is so seldom done is because it is not realized how easy the upkeep would be; how the ventilation and atmosphere need be different only in its moisture from that of the rooms of the house, and how also the introduction of just such a spot constantly freshens the dryness of the atmosphere in the rooms on each side of it. Masses of large ferns or even an aisle of bay trees can be very easily arranged if the side lights are right, and with an attractive background formed by an enclosed colonnade, an introduction of this kind might be of great value, even if no further elaboration of plant growth were used.

The most delightful greenhouse-treatment that I ever saw was on an old Colonial place in New England, where a detached conservatory lay a short distance from the house proper and was reached through a curved pleached walk of hornbeam leading from the side doorway of the house. In this large greenhouse every law — I imagine — of typical construction in shape, angles, and size had been disregarded at the time of its building. The roof was glass in this case, the top light subdued, yet playing through the interlaced leafage of plant-growth which spread over one's head. One suddenly stepped into a delicious, warm, fresh dampness of air, the silence broken by fairy sounds of insects and the twitter of birds. A perfume from the blooms and the changing glint of sunshine through the green lent so the sense of summer that the deep snow outside, in the northern winter, seemed impossible in contrast.

I wish I might describe the impression that this never-to-be-forgotten spot left, this example of what a greenhouse can be — this one, which required comparatively small upkeep. I remember it as being at least fifty feet in diameter, round or octagonal in shape, the side glass not over nine feet in height and the roof rising slightly to a central peak, perhaps fourteen feet high at its centre. The ground, where not hidden by plants, was covered by little crunching pebbles. Comfortable and delightfully shaped chairs and tables were ready for one's use. A water basin with a few pond lilies and water tulips lay in the centre, round in shape, but its edge was informally broken by ivy and a few jonquils. The plants were all growing from the soil itself. Cherokee roses unfurled their extraordinarily beautiful single white blooms from shoots on wood the size of one's forearm, which stretched out in horizontal runners to twenty or thirty feet in side- and top-growth. The new twigs and young buds of the various plants stood out in the damp, warm air and birds flitted here and there among the branches. White jasmine, heliotrope, and orange trees vied with each other in their abundance of perfume. One allamanda plant stretched across the side and the top of this enclosure, making in its rampant growth and exquisite bloom the inspiration for a thousand designs in form and color. The hum of bees pervaded the place, and one's sense of tranquil leisure found a counterpart in the lazy, graceful movements of the goldfish in the pool. There was a bewitching and unexpected confusion of different interlacing blooms. The enchanting formation of young leaves and tight buds made the bark of the old vines delightful in contrast — some of a grayish green, others of a cinnamon brown — and the reddish leaves of young rose-shoots combined to make marvelous color. The ground-covering of the planted space was very lush in its growth and unexpectedly "tufty" with English ivy, which was evidently kept well pinched off where not needed. In other places this indefatigable climber and traveler moused its way into dark, damp recesses and then, after making delectable, full, soft growth in some neglected corner, struck up toward the light, growing greener and more transparent in its color, and so on up until some piece of framework or some branching woody plant was found. When out of bounds, the gardener undoubtedly restrained its reckless progress and brought it back to where it could do no mischief. Plants are so like children: so many of them climb everything that presents itself and stand in the same need of a gentle understanding hand which can restrain. To check their adventure too strenuously tears away a growth of individual development which may deprive the world of a wonderful expression of beauty, with children as with plants alike.

A second doorway led from this round enclosure of bloom to a very long well-pruned vista of grapes in an adjoining greenhouse, springing, as did the other plants, from the natural grade — as the greenhouse held no commonly-found benches. The vines met overhead with a symmetry of outline which came from years of well-considered and careful pruning. The arch was Gothic in form and exquisite in composition and color, seen in perspective from the doorway of the flowered space as well as at closer range.

In this enclosed New England "winter garden," as we might call it, there was a luxurious sense of aloofness in its beauty and its age. The place forbade your even thinking of modern life outside, which seemed by contrast very crude and lacking in margin. Values suddenly assumed different and new proportions of importance, and the goal of life was utterly transformed.

On our way back to the house the snow lay white and deep outside, and the black branches of the hornbeam were like a Seymour Haden etching clean-cut in line against the snow. This must all be recalled, alas, as a distant memory, for the chance of going again to renew the delight of it all is forever gone. Like so much of its kind, it has been torn down and obliterated in the " march of improvement " by new owners.

With a knowledge of the exquisite natural growth of our *Azalea calendulacea* of the South or our northern white *Azalea viscosa* or pinxter flower (*Azalea nudiflora*), it is incredible to think of the fashion that has crushed down upon this species of plant through pruning, when grown in hybrid form for commercial use. The freedom of branch, the grace of the woody twigs, and the exquisite texture of the young green shoots with the blooms poised like so many butterflies, should certainly defy the fashion of pinching back until a mass of color is produced which looks as if it were pasted over the almost leafless mushroom shape—which has as completely lost its semblance to an azalea plant as the bloom has lost its relationship to a flower. Our commercial growers have much to learn in the grace and picturesque quality of the free-growing azalea. When it is realized that the same old plants may be treasured by owners and made to rebloom each year with ever-increasing beauty and luxuriance, they will not find their way into the scrap heap as " finished."

An experiment was once made of turning a great top-room in a city house into a breakfast-room and conservatory combined. The walls were heavily grown with *Ficus repens*, jasmine, and ivy. Two gay parrots lent a festive air to this light spot, and the simple bulbs — raised with little skill or trouble by all the children in the family — found their places here. It turned out to be a never-ending source of delight on winter days, and being high up, was cut off from the noise of the street below. It is extraordinary that greater use is not made of the top-space which is often available in good-sized city houses. The light is quite valuable for this purpose, and variety is made in the general home-environment. Interesting tiles for walls and floors can be used; wall fountains can be easily introduced; the great window-spaces not only provide fine high-lights but give far greater advantage in outlook to sky and distance than any other windows in the house. The glass, being made of many small leaded panes, becomes by no means an unimportant feature in the decoration. The heating may be arranged to be practically inconspicuous and is of easy control in a modern house. What a place, in the heart of a city, to have for the forced plants of almond and azalea, brought from the utilitarian greenhouse, to find themselves suddenly transformed, like Cinderella, in a beautiful setting. Calla lilies might bloom and besport themselves with characteristic grace and boldness, with blue water-hyacinths growing tranquilly at their base in the basins of the wall fountains. If one liked fuchsias, amazing espalier-effects could be made with old and trained plants, as with heliotrope and geraniums. These plants form great trusses of woody stems and increase in beauty as they grow older year by year. Nothing is more tragic than the annual waste of these plants. They are destroyed by the thousands in mere infancy; only when "grown up" do these plants show what they really can be in their characteristic growth.

One delightful old gentleman that I knew, one of the rarest of people, loved nothing better than to walk between the benches of his green-houses, admiring the great masses of cinerarias, gloxinias, and primulas. But the satisfaction was incomplete, for he longed to bring the bloom up into his library. He wanted, however, more of it than the room could hold within reason, so one entire end of the room was converted — by a series of sliding doors made of very beautifully proportioned panes of glass — into an enclosed space beyond, which was completely filled with all the luxuriance and blaze of color that this old flower-lover could have packed into it. He could not get enough; he loved it in masses, as so many people do. He would stand for ten minutes at a time looking into a bank of primulas and yet turn away unsatisfied, with a sigh. Purples, magentas, gorgeous cyclamen colors, tulips in profusion, found their way into the lower spaces, and acacia, genista, and white oleander in great abundance towered into the air, intermingling their bloom with orchids which were introduced in any available spot. It was not in the least beautiful in composition. It was absolutely the product of his gardener's skill and his own old-fashioned taste. The simplicity and sombreness in color of the book-filled room and the unbridled lavishness of the flower-filled space practically enclosed in it were a complete disclosure of a most delightful contrast in the tastes of the owner.

If a regular greenhouse must be had for purely utilitarian purposes, it should be borne in mind that it no more belongs in the public sight than a well-equipped flower-room or sewing-room is in evidence in the house. Many a beautiful and well-planned place has been ruined by the introduction of a greenhouse where it should not have been seen. On the very old places the choice of site often seems to have been much happier than on many modern places, for we are apt to find lean-to greenhouses placed against some high stone or brick wall. Perhaps these old ones are now less in evidence because time itself has slowly (and slyly) been growing great pine-branches or other tree-forms across their outline, and the semiscreening, having once introduced itself, is not readily cut down; whereas on the new place the tree-planting with which one would like to screen a greenhouse from sight meets with every form of objection on the part of the gardener and owner. They clamor for absolutely unbroken light for the plants, but fail in the vision to see what this structure of glass does — in bad composition — to the effect of the whole scheme.

GREENHOUSES

Where a group of forcing-houses had in one instance to exist and a garden had to be planted in its immediate vicinity, a greenhouse forecourt was formed, bounded by a very high clipped hedge of *Salix pentandra*, the openings in it being clipped in vaulted shape where garden paths passed through. This hedge cut off the greenhouses completely from the garden, and the background formed by the hedge offered an extremely good termination for that end of the garden. A hedge of this description can be used as a screen without cutting off the necessary light from the greenhouses if it is placed some thirty to fifty feet away, thus forming a very valuable semishaded court between the hedge and the glass buildings, where winter-blooming plants find an ideal place to rest through the summer. Flowers in pots during their resting period, either sunk or on the surface, are easily cared for and give that charming note of summer potted confusion that one finds so commonly in the gardens of France and Italy. A court of this description may also be found useful in carting material to the gardens, if there is no other approach for this purpose, space being provided to have a cart turned and backed up at will.

Spasmodic attempts at more bearable architectural lines have been made of late, and the planning of greenhouse entrances and better roof-treatment in some cases has been attempted; but architects must deal with this, as it is their province, and perhaps the future will not hold the problems in " planting out," which to-day confront one with the usual greenhouse.

WÀTER
~in~the
GÀRDEN

VI

WATER IN THE GARDEN

ATER in the planning of a garden plays as great a part, in its placing and use, as any other detail. Whether for its reflection or for its sound, to introduce water is to include the fantastic and the intangible, and a garden without it is robbed of poetry and romance. Its subtle effect upon us is far greater than we know in counteracting our sense of parching heat; and we not only feast our eyes on the exquisite reflections and our ears on the varied sounds of its making, but are refreshed by the impression of its life-giving moisture. The reflections more than double the beauty of garden detail; an ample pool with plenty of space about it both fulfills the opportunity for a perfect point in garden design and gives one the impression of starting anew with every path which may lead from it; whereas the same point in the garden, if planted to flowers or turf only, makes one feel each path leading from it is a monotonous repetition in planted space.

Water pools in private gardens are almost always too small and too deep. Their margins should be simple in form, and the plantings made about them carefully trained in broken masses of woody plants and vines. Without any apparent study, just enough green growth may be introduced to sweep down and into the water and to cover the top of the coping to perhaps two thirds of its entire surface. To completely cover the margin of a pool is to create a monotonous wreath. If a coping has a reason for existing, it has a reason for being seen, and it should be of a material which is improved not only by age but by moisture. Its inside edge may be so formed as to make a perfect shallow bathing-rim for birds which find no place to besport themselves in the rest of the pool on account of its depth : in this way great varieties of bird-life are enticed to the garden.

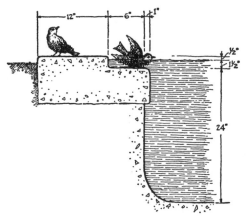

Since the reflection lends so much, it is well to have a pool large enough to reflect the extreme height of a single spreading dogwood or mass of arborvitæ or high azaleas, which might be planted close to its edge. The reflection of a group of cedars, for example, brings a vertical line double the height of the trees into the composition and so relieves the monotony of the horizontal surface of water- and garden-level. How many times have we all seen naked garden-pools in centres of elaborate though monotonously planted gardens, and have felt that the pool suggested nothing more than a sunken tub only reflecting a patch of unbroken sky — a watery grave for toads. We often find an inferior fountain placed in its centre, making the one crude interruption in the garden's lack of height in planting.

Garden-makers of the Old World, especially in Spain and Italy, set us an extraordinary example in the importance of water. The long canals of the Spanish gardens — with their reflection of overhanging and interlaced green — need no reminder; in Italy again and again water finds its way, by a most systematic use, from the reservoir on the highest point of the property down through a series of water-features to the final distribution, when it is used for irrigation in the drier areas below. The reservoir of the Villa Falconieri in Frascati, for instance, so generally known and so beautiful as a detail in itself, is but the high starting-point for a series of uses to which that water is put. Cascades fall from one level to another, and after flowing to basins where the water lies filled with lazy reflection, rise again in fountains below. It is utilized in various decorative ways and finally in irrigation. Part of the overflow is often piped in one direction for the house-supply, while the rest of the surplus water is used in quite another section of the property, or to form a swimming-pool. To make use of various levels, letting them play hand in hand with the frolic of running water, is like turning loose two congenial spirits who create their own reason for existing in the most fascinating and playful of moods. We seldom use water in the profusion found in Italy, though we have it so often in great unharnessed abundance. In the variety of schemes where the same water may be utilized in its flow from level to level we have still much to learn and adopt from the examples of the Old World.

In informal gardens the introduction either of a stream of water or of a small pond is well worth considering. If an existing stream can possibly be used, it is well to introduce it in selecting the garden-site, even though some difficult and careful planting is necessary in relating its position to that of the house. It will pay in the long run to have one's flower space include this natural flow of water, which will form the very centre of interest when it is developed, to say nothing of its benefit in irrigation. Parched and painfully stereotyped flower-gardens are often placed in the uninviting glare of a clear, unbroken summer sky, when not many yards away runs a little stream which — if judiciously dammed in places and treated with careful planting and well-managed marginal effect — might have been the nucleus for the creation of an enchanting flower-enclosure, full of every condition of light, shade, and degree of moisture for various plants: a place, in fact, which would have been a pleasure and an inspiration; whereas the actual, existing garden, in conventional, unimaginative relation to the house, lends no invitation to seedling, bird, or man!

Having but a small stream of water, a pond of no mean size can be made in connection with one's garden, and by the introduction of a few ducks, the pleasures derived from it are never-ending. The whole drama of fresh-water life which can exist in a small area is enacted here. This body of water draws into the scene of the garden many birds which one's pond-less neighbor can never entice, and the Wagnerian undertone of insect life on a summer night is more than doubled. Ducks in themselves are quite harmless and make the most amazing pilgrimages about the turf paths and regions around the pond. Especially at dusk they march in single file in quest of food, reminding one of the inevitable picture-book of our youth which always said " quack-quack, quack-quack " in rhyme with " come-back, come-back." They seem to like paths in their pilgrimages as no other animal is considerate enough to do, and the goldfish and frogs in the pond are very much more interesting to them as food than anything our gardens have to offer.

Many times water is allowed to flow too silently. In the case of the overflow from some spring or reservoir, it is well to make an artificial interruption even if it is not seen, thus adding much in sound to the garden or terrace which may be in close proximity to it. If it can be seen, so much the better.

WATER IN THE GARDEN

Special emphasis may be valuable in pointing out the unnecessary, hard margins we commonly see where small bodies of water, like streams or ponds, have been created as features of use or of decoration. Not only should there be planting of some height at advantageous positions, but a judicious massing of lower and spreading forms of shrubs which would clothe the edge in branches leaning well over and into the water. Clethra, benzoin, willows, flags, and azaleas belong to these natural margins, and a few pond lilies and some lotus which bring the effect of planting well out into the water. The latter are greedy plants and take full possession wherever they are allowed. This should be guarded against or too great a proportion of the clear water surface will be covered. To prevent this, they may be planted in tubs or boxes in shallow ponds with natural bottoms or in cement pools. The earth can in this way be as rich as necessary and their spreading too much is prevented. When a pond is shallow only about its margins, there is no danger in planting lilies along portions of its banks in the natural bottom, for the depth of the water, if sufficient, will of itself check their wandering.

Swimming-pools surrounded by poplars, with the reflection of finely shaped cement seats, might find their way into the proximity of gardens far more often than they do. It is not in the least necessary to associate the idea of the swimming-pool with the crude masonry tanks we usually find, devoid of every bit of beauty they might lend, either in themselves as reflecting pools or as a setting for the children who bathe in them. Why should a swimming-pool lie entirely open to the sky when part of it might be in shadow?

Many an owner whose property bordered on the Italian lakes has had his problem to meet in boat-landings, boat-houses, and approaches to the higher land surrounding the house proper, and in many cases wonderfully picturesque arrangements have been produced. The Villa Arconati or Balbianello, on Lake Como, boasts two landings, one for calm weather and another one, more protected, for rougher days and for the mooring of little boats. Roses in profusion mingle with the green of outstretching boughs on coping and balustrade, and are reflected in lavishness of color by the lapping waters beneath them. Interesting posts for lanterns and others for moorings are all exquisitely planned, and add new features to the harmony and reason of the utilitarian yet picturesque boat-landing. Everything is of one note: the combination of usefulness and luxury influenced by a true understanding of the importance of beauty, which enters into the demands for the setting of daily life in so many of the Italian lake villas.

Do we find this same note very often in the treatment of our water-fronts, where property is bordered by rivers or sheltered coves? We all know any number of crude and unimaginative approaches to boat-houses. Abrupt wooden steps and a cheap handrail are not uncommon approaches to boat-landings and bath-houses on many elaborately planned and important places. This incongruity of ugly bath-houses and makeshift landings is impossible to understand. Our water-fronts are rare where any really picturesque planning and architectural care have gone to their making, and yet no more exquisite natural sites are available the world over. The opportunities for creating delightful effects through combinations of architecture, judicious plantings, and water seem to have escaped many owners. Occasionally in well-planned camps these features are above the average, because the preponderance of shore-front growth in its native luxuriance defies crudity. It is on the more open river- and lake-fronts that more attention might be given and beautiful arrangements be gained.

WATER IN THE GARDEN

The mere thought of water and its uses, æsthetic and utilitarian, suggests unending schemes in one's mind, and the many lost opportunities for its use are hard to forgive. The arbor which holds no wall fountain, the vacant spots in gardens where bird baths might find their places, the swallows and the red-winged black birds that find no pond in which to dip at sundown, and the unbroken silence where falling water might be at all times heard — make one fairly cry aloud to wake the visionless owners to what might be theirs.

IN CONCLUSION

THERE is so much that might be said by an abler pen than mine, that, in closing, I realize each topic has been but lightly touched upon, playing mostly, as it were, on the high notes of imagination.

Perhaps those who care, finding a keynote, will respond through their own vibrations with deeper reverberating tones, which shall produce a harmony of purpose for greater ends than I have been able to voice.

This imagination of ours — the medium through which the creative works, with its undreamed-of heights and depths — is ever proving that it moves in waves, bringing to life again and again the impulse and energy which have produced so much that is fine!

"Beauty old, yet ever new,
Eternal Voice and Inward Word."

183

VILLA ARCONATI OR BALBIANELLO ON LAKE COMO

OPEN BOAT–LANDING ON THE LAKE EDGE, USED IN CALM WEATHER.
SEE PAGE 182

185

VILLA ARCONATI

VILLA ARCONATI, LAKE COMO

TERRACE, SHOWING USE OF EXTREME EDGE OF PROPERTY OVERHANGING THE
LAKE

VILLA ARCONATI OR BALBIANELLO: LAKE COMO
THE SHORE FORMATION OUTSIDE THE LITTLE HARBOR SHOWN BELOW

THE PROTECTED LANDING. SEE PAGE 182

HEADLANDS
RELATION BETWEEN THE FLOWER GARDEN AND LAKE CHAMPLAIN

UNDERCLIFF

THE BIRD BATH. FIGURE BY FRANCES GRIMES, SCULPTOR

BRICK HOUSE

GARDEN POOL : SHOWING IMPORTANCE OF INCIDENTAL PLANTING ABOUT POOL-
MARGIN, TO RELIEVE HARD LINE OF COPING

CROWHURST

THE SEA IN RELATION TO THE GARDEN FLOWERS HIGH ABOVE IT

CROWHURST

ILLUSTRATING THE ADVANTAGE OF LEAVING ADEQUATE CLEAR WATER–SUR-
FACE, WHEN LILIES ARE PLANTED IN GARDEN POOLS. THE REFLECTIONS OF
THE PINES BEYOND WOULD BE LOST IF THIS POINT HAD NOT BEEN OBSERVED

CROWHURST

THE GARDEN AND SEA BEYOND, FROM AN UPPER WINDOW

MERCHISTON FARM

THE POND, A PLAYGROUND FOR DUCKS AND CHILDREN, TAKEN SEVEN YEARS
AFTER PLANTING. SEE PAGE 180

MERCHISTON FARM

THE POND, SEEN FROM THE FLOWER GARDEN

MERCHISTON FARM

THE POND, EIGHT YEARS AFTER PLANTING. SEE AXIS H ON PLAN, PAGE 52

MERCHISTON FARM

SITE OF THE POND WHEN FIRST MADE, BEFORE ANY PLANTING OF IMPORTANCE
HAD BEEN ADDED TO ITS HARD MARGINS. SEE PAGE 194

MERCHISTON FARM

THE POND THREE YEARS AFTER PLANTING. WILLOW CUTTINGS WERE RUN INTO
THE SOFT BANKS AND ROOTED QUICKLY, FORMING A FINE NATURAL GROWTH.
CLETHRA, IRIS PSEUDACORUS, GERMAN IRIS, AND BENZOIN (OR SPICE BUSH)
ALSO ARE USED NEAR THE MARGIN

UNDERCLIFF

THE HOUSE-TERRACE AND THE SEA BROUGHT TOGETHER BY CAREFUL ELIM-
INATION OF MANY TREES, LEAVING JUST ENOUGH FOREGROUND TO GIVE THE
PROPER BALANCE AND COMPOSITION. SEE AXIS B, PAGE 11

UNDERCLIFF

A STONE BATH–HOUSE BUILT OF THE NATIVE ROCK. THE SUBSTANTIAL WOODEN
LATTICE OVER THE ROOF WAS BUILT TO HOLD WILD GRAPEVINES, MAKING THE
INTRODUCTION OF THE BUILDING PRACTICALLY INCONSPICUOUS FROM THE
LEVELS ABOVE AND FROM THE WATER

UNDERCLIFF

LOOKING STRAIGHT OUT TO SEA FROM ITS WOODLAND SETTING
SEE AXIS C, PAGE 11
(THE LATE HERBERT D. HALE, ARCHITECT)

WELWYN

THE GARDEN REFLECTIONS IN THE POOL

WELWYN

IN THE GARDEN

WELWYN

THE GARDEN POOL

WELWYN

THE GARDEN POOL. THE DIAL MARKS AN IMPORTANT MAJOR-AXIS AND THE
REFLECTIONS DOUBLE THE VERTICAL LINES OF TREES

MAUDESLEIGH

AN OLD ITALIAN WALL–FOUNTAIN IN THE GARDEN

LOST OPPORTUNITY FOR BEAUTIFUL TREATMENT OF APPROACH
TO THE OCEAN AND OF SETTING FOR A GOOD BATH–HOUSE

SEE PAGE 182

A PICTURESQUE GROWTH OF TREES WHICH EVENTUALLY EM-
BELLISHED A FLIGHT OF STONE STEPS LEADING TO A BOAT PIER

TYPICAL OF MANY BATH–HOUSES AND BOAT–LANDINGS ON
PRIVATE ESTATES OF IMPORTANCE

OLDFIELDS

PLANTING OF THE POOL–MARGIN, PARTIALLY COVERED WITH VINES AND
AZALEAS, BRINGING THE COPING AND WATER TOGETHER

OLDFIELDS

HARDY AZALEAS OVERHANGING THE POOL–MARGIN

OLDFIELDS

SHOWING THE COPING OF THE POOL BEFORE IT HAD BEEN SUFFICIENTLY
PLANTED OUT

OLDFIELDS

THE LITTLE GREEN GARDEN IN AN ANGLE OF THE HOUSE, SEEN FROM THE
GARDEN OF LARGER SCALE

OLDFIELDS

TAKING ADVANTAGE OF A WATERFRONT AS A SITE FOR HOUSE,
GARDEN, BOAT-HOUSE, AND LANDING COMBINED AS A UNIT

VILLA PALMIERI, NEAR FLORENCE

USE OF WATER IN INNER COURT

VILLA PALMIERI

THE PAVILION OVERHANGING THE SWIMMING-POOL

VILLA PALMIERI

SWIMMING POOL

VILLA CONTI, FRASCATI

THE ELABORATE WATER-CASCADE FORMS THE MAIN FEATURE OF AN IM-
PORTANT AXIS, SEEN ACROSS THE FORECOURT THROUGH A VISTA OF LIVE OAKS

VILLA CONTI, FRASCATI

THE WATER SEEN FROM THE TERRACE ABOVE THE FORECOURT, AS IT RISES
AGAIN IN FOUNTAINS BELOW

VILLA FALCONIERI, FRASCATI

THE DECORATIVE FEATURE MADE IN THE WALL OF THE RESERVOIR DAM
AS SEEN FROM BELOW

VILLA FALCONIERI, FRASCATI
THE DAM FROM THE RESERVOIR

VILLA FALCONIERI, FRASCATI

THE RESERVOIR, THE HIGHEST POINT, FROM WHICH THE WATER FLOWS TO
LOWER LEVELS. SEE PAGE 179

INDIAN NECK

A SMALL FOUNTAIN IN THE CENTRE OF THE GARDEN

A GARDEN IN GRANADA

HAMPTON COURT

THE VALUE OF AXIS IN BRINGING THE VISTAS OF GREEN INTO RELATION WITH
WATER AND BUILDINGS

HAMPTON COURT

NEARER DETAIL, SHOWING TREATMENT IN BOTH DIRECTIONS, IN SPACE
BETWEEN FOUNTAIN AND PALACE

HAMPTON COURT

FOUNTAIN AS SEEN THROUGH IMPORTANT DOORWAY

SOSIEGO

POND ON THE ESTATE OF MRS. DANIEL LORD, LAWRENCE, LONG ISLAND, MADE
ARTIFICIALLY SOME FORTY YEARS AGO

SOSIEGO

ANOTHER VIEW OF THE POND, WITH ITS BEAUTY IN REFLECTED WEEPING
WILLOWS

GUY'S CLIFF, NEAR WARWICK, ENGLAND
NEAR ENOUGH TO THE RIVER TO USE THE VALUE OF ITS REFLECTING SURFACE

A LONG CURVED WALK ON THE SHORE OF MASSACHUSETTS, PLANTED WITH
FLOWERS, SHRUBS, AND TREES THAT ARE UNHURT BY SALT-WATER EXPOSURE